# More Praise for This Book

"In my experience, mentoring is one of the strategies for both mentees and mentors effective program is always more challenging than it seems is an invaluable resource for creating the conditions for successful, high-impact mentoring relationships."

—Erica Freedman, Vice President, Talent and Organizational
Development, Day & Zimmermann

"In today's world, where the career-minded need a 'personal board of directors,' mentors need to do more—much more—than just share experiences. Wendy Axelrod's guidance will help you establish effective relationships so you will be a beacon to guide your mentee's development. I wish I'd had this book when I started mentoring!"

—Barbara Jamelli-Sefchik,
Global Head of Career Development, SAP

"*10 Steps to Successful Mentoring* is the ultimate mentoring handbook. Wendy Axelrod has distilled her years of research and practice into an actionable road map that takes out all the guesswork. Filled with assessments, checklists, templates, and more, this book provides the strategies mentors need to develop others, and support their own ongoing development as well."

—Julie Winkle Giulioni, Co-Author,
*Help Them Grow or Watch Them Go*

"Wendy Axelrod's new book *10 Steps to Successful Mentoring* is the ultimate guide to creating a successful mentoring program. Her structured approach not only provides the 'what to do,' but more importantly the 'how,' along with stories, tips, suggestions, and practical tools to help create a terrific mentoring experience for both mentor and mentee."

—Fred Test, VP, Wealth Planning & Advice, TD Wealth

"Through her extensive experience and research, Wendy Axelrod has created a practitioner's field guide for any mentor or mentoring program manager. Most information available on mentoring has been fragmented and theoretical, but this book provides a comprehensive compilation of best practices and tools that any new or experienced mentor can readily apply."

—Tom Kaney, Managing Partner, McKnight Kaney LLC
Former SVP Human Resources, North America,
GlaxoSmithKline Pharmaceuticals

"*10 Steps to Successful Mentoring* is an excellent guide for anyone who wants to start a program (individually or organizationally) or improve the quality of mentoring already in place. It engages the mentor to learn these steps by laying out the significant benefits they will receive. This is a must-have tool for building remarkable, development-producing mentoring relationships."

—Dave Desch, SVP and Chief Human Resources Officer,
C3i Solutions, an HCL Technologies Company

"Mentoring can be one of the most rewarding experiences of our lives. In this terrific book, talent development guru Wendy Axelrod lays out the ultimate road map for mentoring success!"

—Jennifer B. Kahnweiler, Author, *The Introverted Leader*

"Wendy Axelrod takes a fresh, conversational approach to the most important aspects of a mentoring relationship."

—Jenn Labin, Author, *Mentoring Programs That Work*

# 10
# Steps to
# Successful
# *Mentoring*

# Wendy Axelrod, PhD

## Foreword by Beverly Kaye

PRESS

Alexandria, VA

ATD Press is an internationally renowned source of insightful and practical information on talent development, training, and professional development.

ATD Press
1640 King Street
Alexandria, VA 22314 USA

Ordering information: Books published by ATD Press can be purchased by visiting ATD's website attd.org/books or by calling 800.628.2783 or 703.683.8100.

Library of Congress Control Number: 2019933790

ISBN-10: 1-949036-48-0
ISBN-13: 978-1-949036-48-0
e-ISBN: 978-1-949036-49-7

**ATD Press Editorial Staff**
Director: Sarah Halgas
Manager: Melissa Jones
Community of Practice Manager, Human Capital: Eliza Blanchard
Developmental Editor: Jack Harlow
Associate Editor: Courtney Cornelius
Text and Cover Design: Darrin Raaum

Printed by BR Printers, San Jose, CA

# CONTENTS

# Tools and Figures

## Tools

## Figures

# Foreword

I had just finished a presentation to a large group of high potential employees and their leaders and was waiting in the lobby of the hotel for my ride to the airport. I watched as two gentlemen from the group briskly walked over to one another and exchanged a big, warm bear hug. I was intrigued since the group was quite formal and I walked over to them and asked how they knew one another. They said, almost in unison, that they were mentor and mentee. Always curious, I asked the mentee what made his mentor so great....he said, without skipping a beat, "he was authentic." Then I asked the mentor what made his mentee so special and he said (also without skipping a beat) "he was hungry." I never forgot those two words, because I think they define a wonderful mentor–mentee relationship and those words can be said about either partner.

Wendy wonderfully provides mentors and mentees with tips, tools, and exercises to fuel the passion behind both of those words. I've read a number of books on mentoring, written on it myself, and designed programs that make it come alive. Wendy does it better. 10 Steps to Successful Mentoring is the best book I've seen on the subject. I believe it can be used by both sides of the partnership.

Wendy and I have been on parallel paths in our work in the people-development arena for years. We are both devoted to our profession and care deeply about learning and sharing what it takes to develop people. Through the professional associations in which we participate (ATD prime among them), we each engage with others to present, discuss, and adapt development practices to the ever changing organizational and work landscape. When Wendy wrote her first book, Make Talent Your Business, it was clear she dove deeply into what develops people best, and what managers need to focus on. She has a decades-long commitment to developing people in house—in organizations where people work, learn, and grow. People grow especially well when the culture, managers, and peers are intentionally focused on development, with attention that is embedded in daily actions. How do organizations cultivate such a growth environment? That is what Wendy and I have been working on, and you will discover much more about it in this book.

Today's workplace is more complex and tougher to navigate than ever before. In addition, over the last few years two notable trends have emerged among job seekers: they are favoring meaning in their work, even more than money; and, they are eager for growth. Mentoring plays an essential role in filling these needs, and can be powerful and life changing for the individuals receiving it. Yet, that's just the beginning of the story. Mentoring can be positioned in organizations to increase performance, engagement and retention... and at little cost. Perhaps the most important benefit to those reading this book, is that when they do it masterfully, mentors receive incredible rewards that reach far beyond the months or years they spend with their mentee.

But, there is a catch. To do it well, there are deliberate skills involved; actions to take, and actions not to take. Many view mentoring as informal, believe anyone can do it, and anything goes. Under the banner of being a mentor, people jump in with advice, present fervent points of view, or ask questions that serve their own interests and curiosities, rather than the desires of those sitting across from them in the conversation. They talk more than they listen, steer not inspire, or provide solutions rather than enable new career enhancing behaviors. The results can be satisfactory, yet often miss out on the bigger possibilities of enduring development and relationships.

Wendy elegantly and expertly informs and inspires us to do this in the best possible way. This book points you in the right direction, deepens your skills, provides real examples, and saves you time. As you read, you will see that the guiding practices provided, the recommended steps and actions, and the myriad of tools and guides are the result of years of roll-up-your-sleeves experience. She takes scores of real mentor scenarios, including her own, and distills what is most important to understand (your own motivation, how self-awareness develops) and what is important to do (leverage experience for development, elevate the power of questions), and makes them most practical for you to apply.

There is so much for the mentee and mentor to consider. Creating a strong foundation leads to a rich and meaningful experience for both of you. So, spend the time to get to know each other, collaboratively set mentee goals for this experience, craft a reliable game plan, and discuss how the two of you will address challenges in your mentoring process. Then, support your mentee to take risks in trying out new mindsets and behaviors, explore bigger perspectives, and "go internal" to understand more about themselves. Create the important habit of reflection and debriefing. One of my mantras is: an assignment not debriefed is not worth doing. Pausing for insights, especially when your mentee feels safe enough to talk about what is on their mind, can create new approaches to problems they face, and increase determination. Their effort to grow will require them to break old habits, bust through obstacles, and boldly take new actions. You will be there to optimistically support them on their changes, as well as keep your eye on progress.

Ask questions, lots of them. And remember that not all questions are created equal. Be both thoughtful and courageous. Know how to ask, how to listen, and if you'd like guidance on what specific questions to ask—take a look at any chapter. Find sample questions for conversations on specific topics such as expanding the methods for your mentee's development or widening your mentee's network of advocates. You will increase your expertise in a process that involves far less telling, problem fixing and opinion sharing, and more about stretching and enabling (similar to what is used by the most seasoned certified coaches). You will offer your mentee resources and tools, and let them go at it. Throughout, Wendy will be your personal guide. Combined with your wisdom and generosity, all of this leads to greater confidence, awareness, and career growth for your mentee.

The growth in the mentoring process goes both ways. As a mentor, this journey is for you, and can be as developmental as it is enjoyable. What would happen if you set your own goals for this mentoring process? You would deepen your mentoring and coaching skills, make discoveries from your mentee's perceptive, and learn more about yourself. Push beyond your comfort zone, and take on inevitable challenges you will face in the process. Throughout the process, continue to look at yourself and use the questions for reflection found throughout the book. And, you need not feel you are alone in the process. Consider leading or participating in a mentor peer group that meets regularly to support each other's mentoring experience.

Adopt the seven guiding principles of successful mentors that wind their way through all the steps. Consider, for example, how you will continuously "create a conversational safety space" and "cultivate a positive and resilient relationship". These guiding principles, and all the advice provided in the book, heighten your presence as a corporate citizen. They inform you not only about being a great mentor, but also about being a great leader who is authentic and hungry. You will see yourself differently and others will too, leading to your own career enhancement, one of the many benefits of being a masterful mentor.

10 Steps to Successful Mentoring distinguishes itself with the depth and breadth of guidance provided to new and seasoned mentors in the most accessible way. There can no longer be the statement "I would love to mentor, but I don't have the time." This book lays it out for you. We are in critical need of this book right now, it is destined to become a classic, and I am most grateful to Wendy for writing it.

Bev Kaye
Author, *Love 'Em or Lose 'Em and Help*
*Them Grow or Watch Them Grow*
Recipient of ATD's Lifetime Achievement Award
February 2019

# Introduction

"You might already know we've been having incredible success with our mentoring program, and it's grown tremendously with each new cycle," Peter, a company senior leader, told Gayle. "And we'd like you to be part of our next cohort. What would you say to becoming a mentor to a rising-star professional?" Gayle took a deep breath. She had heard great press about the program, but never considered joining.

Gayle had always prided herself on being a team player, sacrificing her own interests to take on new projects. As an engineer for a large software company near Philadelphia, she had thrown herself into her work for more than a decade. She had even passed up a new management opportunity, committed to seeing her project and team through to the finish line of a significant new product offering. Only recently had she begun to worry if she'd made a mistake. "When," Gayle wondered, "will I get the chance to invest in myself?"

Mulling it over for a few moments, Gayle shared her reservations. "My life is already filled with taking care of others. I manage one group, and, as you know, I'm also leading our latest offering, which launches in a few months. I have two children at home, plus I'm helping my dad find a new place to live. Mentoring hardly fits the bill of my next big experience. Not to sound selfish, but if I take on something new right now, it should be something I can do for myself—to learn, feel enriched, and sink my teeth into."

"Precisely!" Peter responded. Gayle didn't understand. Mentoring, she assumed, would simply mean more work for her; yet another person to give herself to, with little in it for her. "This mentoring process has much more to it than you probably realize," Peter added, recognizing the confusion in Gayle's expression. "Yes, it's an opportunity to develop a fellow professional. But it's also an opportunity to invest in yourself. I know when I served as a mentor two years ago, I discovered my tendency was to solve every problem my mentee had, rather than listen—really listen. Then I learned to ask important questions and help him figure it out on his own, and even help him become more self-aware and take some leaps forward in challenges he faced. I got a lot out of exploring things from his vantage point; it was all totally eye-opening for me. That's what we've been building here—an environment where not only mentees, but also mentors, are supported to enhance their skills and learn more about themselves. In fact, we have mentors who *insist* on being included for each new round of the program."

Suddenly, Gayle was intrigued. She had, after all, been looking for a fresh adventure—the cycling club and woodworking classes hadn't cut it. She left her meeting with Peter undecided; maybe becoming a mentor was just what she needed. What would she do?

## Substantial Rewards Await You

The best mentoring leaves a positive and enduring impact on the mentee. It provides the mentee a secure environment to explore aspirations, think more broadly, and behave with far greater effectiveness. But while the process of mentoring typically focuses on the mentee, this book is fervently and enthusiastically dedicated to you . . . the mentor.

The most seasoned and successful mentors know it is not their expertise and years of problem solving that create the basis for their best work as a mentor. It is much more about *how* they engage their mentee, requiring mentors to learn and apply specific growth-promoting approaches. Those focused methods are what led to their mentee's outstanding development. In fact, an important study of company mentoring programs shows that the level of support and learning mentors receive correlates with the level of the results achieved in their mentoring (ATD 2017). Discovering new development methods not only increases your skill, but it also leads to considerably better results for your mentee—a win-win. Increasing your capabilities as a mentor is what this book is all about.

The investment you make to become an outstanding mentor will pay big dividends, beyond the wonderful satisfaction of just helping another. Brenda Dear, the former HR executive with IBM who revitalized their multimillion-dollar mentoring program, is a breathing Wikipedia of the benefits of mentoring for mentors as well as their companies. Both fortunate and grateful for her years of mentoring, she viewed it as crucial in her career—an opportunity to share and learn across job functions, cultures, and generations. Said Brenda: "Mentoring provided me the opportunity to remain connected, to stay relevant, and to be a valuable contributor to the organization" (MentorCloud 2014).

No question, mentoring is very gratifying; and with more mentoring relationships accumulated over time, you will find an expansion of benefits accrued. Based upon research and my years of experience, here are the primary benefits mentors report:

- **Enhance your career.** Mentors get good practice and fine-tune skills such as listening, asking thought-provoking questions, facilitating change, influencing, and overcoming obstacles. Look closely, and you'll notice that these skills are the same required to be an exceptional leader. Your willingness to mentor will get the attention of others, whether in your company or elsewhere, and can lead to offers of broader opportunities. A well-researched and frequently cited study from Sun Microsystems indicates that those being mentored are not the only ones who move up in their career; mentors also were five times more likely to receive increased salary grades than their nonmentoring peers (Morrison 2014).

- **Learn what it takes to develop others.** Committing to this role means you are dedicated to develop someone in significant ways. Your mentee's lasting growth requires myriad developmental actions you will need to take: recognizing your mentee's strengths and weaknesses, identifying what new skills will be learned, addressing obstacles, expanding perspectives, testing new behaviors, reflecting on impact, and perfecting their skills through repeated application. Outside of your daily role, mentoring becomes a safe place to try new developmental approaches without the scrutiny of organizational requirements and policies. You grow as you help another develop.

- **Stay relevant.** Methods, research, and tools change in every discipline over time; the pace seems to get faster and faster. The change, for example, could mean a greater focus on analytics, or use of new communications protocols for working with internal clients. If you have a decade or more of experience and your mentee has less, you can learn from what is currently happening in your field at the ground level. You may also gain knowledge about personal attributes mentees need to have, such as greater flexibility in a world less certain than the one you had earlier in your career. As an example, John Barrows is keenly focused on staying relevant and relies on Morgan, who is 16 years younger, to help educate him. "I grew up and still live in a Microsoft world (PC, Word, Excel, PowerPoint), which Morgan's generation views as archaic. So he's teaching me (forcing me) to use Google Docs, Slack, and other collaborative tools, not only to improve our communication but also to help me work more effectively with others in his cohort and to be more relevant in their eyes" (Barrows 2017).

- **Gain new perspectives.** Through the numerous conversations with your mentee about carrying out their daily responsibilities, you will learn their values and perspectives on many aspects of work life and life as a whole. Whether the two of you have dissimilarities due to different backgrounds, upbringing, education, or generation, consider this your opportunity to challenge the way you typically look at things and expand your own world view. Seeing familiarities in a new light will broaden your possibilities. Learning from your mentee and appreciating their way of thinking actually increases your mutual trust and respect. I received a comment from a mentor during a pulse survey that typifies how mentors view this: "Viewing the world through others' eyes continues to strengthen my strategic value."

- **Learn more about yourself.** During conversations with your mentee, "listen" to what questions you are asking, what assumptions you are making, what you find disturbing in the conversations, and what advice you offer. Use this for self-reflection. What do all of these say about you: your interests, your ways of operating, and your "go-to" ideas? And, more directly, you can ask mentee for feedback; seeing yourself from their perspective can be quite revealing.

## Reaching New Heights as a Mentor

During my junior year in college, I realized that my life's ambition was to work with people to help them become their most accomplished self. While my fellow psychology-major peers were headed into clinical psychology, I veered in another direction. Though scarcely knowing what it was all about, I dove into a deep learning, gaining an education and experiences to attain a PhD in organizational psychology. What I loved about that period was leveraging the classes and concepts during my consulting work conducted with my major professors, learning from experience and with others. The learning gained was not simply in my head, it was also in my gut, my hands, and in my bones! I was passionate about developing others, but not simply based on book learning. What followed was years devoted to organizational, leader, and people development, as well as original research with Jeannie Coyle about how some managers were truly exceptional at developing their people. All that culminated in our book *Make Talent Your Business: How Exceptional Managers Develop People While Getting Results* (Axelrod and Coyle 2011).

The enduring fascination with development seeped into my volunteer life. As president of a human resources association in Greater

Philadelphia (now Philadelphia Society for People and Strategy), I initiated and led a mentoring program for early-in-career professionals, now in its 17th year, graduating scores of mentees who have gone onto highly successful careers. Along with my colleagues who helped to implement the program, and as mentors ourselves, we learned and experimented with what really made the biggest impact for mentee and mentor growth (Axelrod 2012). It has been an incredible playground for learning and uncovering what occurs in superb mentoring and how to achieve remarkable outcomes.

Mentoring others is not to be taken lightly; we have a significant responsibility and enormous influence. Continuing to grow and develop ourselves not only enriches our mentees, but it also enhances our relationships at work and at home. With a positive ripple effect, the better we become at mentoring, the more the world around us also changes for the better. Like finding a superb high-yield mutual fund, the investment we make in our own development pays big dividends, and we get to share that with others.

## How to Use This Book

If you have mentored before or if this is your first time, from this book you will learn how to unlock your own motivations for mentoring, collaboratively shape a learning contract, establish a relationship of trust, and confidently ask thought-provoking questions that help your mentees see a new path. You will discover how to use a variety of learning approaches with your mentees, apply psychology and neuroscience with your mentee to uncover insights, leverage day-to-day work experiences as a learning lab, and more. As a result, you will provide a safe and rich environment for in-depth conversations that readies your mentee to take risks, try new behaviors, and reach for bigger aspirations. The outcome of this type of mentoring is a path to increased capabilities, heightened self-awareness, confidence with courageous actions, and gratifying career growth.

*10 Steps to Successful Mentoring* is filled with scores of tools, models, and questions that will give you encouragement to use new methods with confidence. You will also find dozens of real examples (with the names and job titles changed), highlighting the approaches that turn mentor challenges into successful results. For the new or seasoned mentor, this book will guide you through the process, but not in a mechanical, cookbook fashion. There can be no "follow these steps, one by one, and every time you will get this fantastic outcome." Every mentee is unique, requiring you to keep your eye on the process as it unfolds, and grow in your own skill set. There will be surprises, frustrations, delights, and unexpected impacts. Learning from the mentoring process in this book promises a lifetime of memorable experiences for your mentee and a lasting legacy for yourself. Plan to not only succeed as a mentor, but also truly excel and change lives.

Here is how the book is organized to support you.

The starting elements of the mentoring, the first three steps, help to create a robust foundation so you and your mentee are positioned for a supportive and deliberate development process.

- **Step 1: Prepare for Your Role.** The role of the mentor is often unintentionally misrepresented in theory and in practice. This chapter distinguishes it from other development-focused roles. It offers seven guiding principles of successful mentoring, which create a basis for your process. It aims to help you understand your motivation to be a mentor and provides a readiness checklist.
- **Step 2: Establish the Relationship.** As in any relationship, the mentor-mentee dynamic necessitates that you get to know each other. This chapter focuses on finding common ground, identifying your roles and expectations, setting the tone for ongoing in-depth work together, and deciding what to cover in the early meetings.
- **Step 3: Set the Direction.** Too many mentoring relationships begin enthusiastically, only to be derailed when mentors and mentees don't establish useful goals. This chapter suggests how mentee goals are shaped to stretch your mentee while also allowing them to have real-time opportunities to apply

what they are learning. It also guides the identification of your own goals, helping you to establish a protocol and structure for your conversations and what will occur between meetings.

The methods and approaches you will use throughout the mentoring process that lead to remarkable results are contained in steps 4 through 7. There is no distinct step-wise order. At one time or another you will need to draw from them all; in fact, several will occur simultaneously in your mentoring conversations. Mastering these methods will set you apart from other mentors and create high impact for your mentee and yourself.

- **Step 4: Leverage Experience for Development.** Experience is a great teacher when it is properly shaped for the right lessons. Help your mentee to examine the possibilities, field-test new approaches, enlist others for insight and feedback, and extract the learning.

- **Step 5: Expand Growth Using Everyday Psychology.** Creating lasting growth needs to be personally geared to the makeup of the individual. The keys are understanding emotions and neuroscience, knowing oneself, knowing your mentee, creating safety, and raising self-awareness.

- **Step 6: Elevate the Power of Questions.** What happens when you formulate the right inquiry, step back, and listen to your mentee? You both end up learning more. This chapter shows you how to construct questions to make them thoughtful, developmental, and engaging, while also gearing them around the different types of learning. It also stresses how to convey challenging questions with respect and compassion, and knowing what questions to ask yourself to become more expert.

- **Step 7: Diversify the Development Methods.** What helps spur development in one mentee may not be the same for others. You will need to understand the right fit for your mentee, tap into the variety of useful development options, and diversify your own development during this process.

Once the relationship is well established and there is a rhythm to the mentoring, push further to truly stretch your mentee and yourself. Your mentee will benefit from influencing others to enrich and widely apply their new skills. There is an opportunity for you to stretch even further too, with a chapter dedicated to helping you address knotty mentoring challenges. Even with persistent obstacles, the best mentors know how create success.

- **Step 8: Promote Influence Skills.** Mentees need to expand their influence abilities the further they take their careers. Help your mentee to recognize influence opportunities and challenges, enhance four crucial influence skills, and progressively strengthen influence.
- **Step 9: Address Mentor Challenges.** Do exceptional mentors write off challenging mentees as unsalvageable? No. They instead see the situation as a golden opportunity to grow. This chapter provides support for neutralizing four mentoring relationship roadblocks, succeeding with mentees who are challenging, and managing outside influencers.

Whether your process has been six months or more than two years, the final elements of your mentoring needs to be as productive as any other step. It solidifies the relationship and lessons learned, and points to direction for the future.

- **Step 10: Consolidate Learning and Bring Closure.** For both mentor and mentee, this is the crucial last phase of the work together and includes steps involved with anticipating closure, individually preparing for the wrap-up conversation, conducting the wrap-up conversation (including what's next), and consolidating the lessons of your own experience as a mentor.

## The Next Step

Now the journey, with this book as your guide, gets underway. In the next chapter you will dive into what it takes to fully prepare for your role as mentor: understanding your role, your motivation, guiding principles, and the typical phases of mentoring. This step lays a foundation for a remarkable experience. You are destined to continually grow as an exceptional mentor!

# Step 1
# Prepare for Your Role

*"Today's preparation determines tomorrow's achievement."–Anonymous*

## Overview

- Recognize your role as a mentor.
- Use the seven guiding principles for successful mentoring.
- Understand your motivation for being a mentor.
- Participate in a program or create your own.
- Consider the readiness checklist.

Supporting career ambitions, boosting confidence, broadening perspective, inspiring big strides, providing safe conversational space, raising awareness, building deep trust, overcoming obstacles, asking growth-provoking questions, encouraging experimentation, increasing another's influence, sustaining momentum for growth, and demonstrating patience for learning . . . who can possibly do all this? You can!

During this mentoring process, you will use the nature of your relationship and tailored conversations as the instrument for growth. Because this is a deliberate development process, you will relinquish power and smart solutions in favor of using approaches that truly allow the mentee to grow. You will meet your mentee where they are today, trading in the direct problem solving and expertise for their experimentation and accumulated confidence. It is a lot to do—but very achievable and yields substantial rewards.

You are up for the journey, want to do the best job possible, and will grow as a result. Bravo!

Whether you have mentored five times or never, whether you are part of an organized program or not, this book is written for you. Are you ready to get started?

## Recognize Your Role as a Mentor

During my career, there have been a couple outstanding individuals who I consider my mentors. These mentors were generous leaders who nurtured me and helped to grow my capabilities, and I was fortunate they took an interest in me. However, I identified them as my mentors only after the fact, after we were into the relationship for months or years, with no discernable start date. The timing of when the relationship moved into mentoring was blurry because I already had an organizational reporting relationship with them (they were executives and I was in the next level down). It was only once they saw my performance and got to know my character that they began going the extra mile to create a more developmental relationship with me. Those relationships helped me understand organizational dynamics and boost my confidence to make bold moves, such as proposing and then leading a significant organization change process at my Fortune 100 company. Their roles as mentors were mitigated because while giving me advice, they also kept the objectives of the corporation in mind. In fact, we never formally stated that this was a mentoring relationship. At the time, I am not even sure how they might have reacted to me calling them my mentors. Would they have been proud? Surprised? Reluctant?

In addition to these leaders, I was fortunate to have a handful of highly talented and trusted colleagues in my field who supported my growth, expanded my knowledge, and helped me to be more courageous. I looked to them for guidance, relied on our stimulating conversations, and really enjoyed having time with them. Yet, we also never had a well-structured process; those ongoing discussions were more off-the-cuff, which seemed appropriate. Looking back, I now realize none of these relationships ever put the mentoring into full gear.

You can and will do even better than my former "mentors." Because your role and path forward will be far more transparent and structured, your mentoring relationships will accomplish career-changing results for your mentee. You will have the true title of mentor and own the responsibility to nurture, inspire, and help drive growth; and happily, you will also enjoy the rewards.

## Describing Your Role as Mentor

In your role as mentor, you are signing on to be a developmental partner for your mentee with a clear structure, ground rules, and a focus that is squarely centered on the mentee's professional growth. That growth will yield greater engagement, enjoyment, confidence, performance, and career development. You make that growth possible by facilitating mutual trust and respect, establishing a safe space to expand, asking thought-provoking questions, co-creating solutions, and suggesting approaches that help them grow.

The quality of your relationship is the primary tool for your work. The relationship is voluntary and "at will" for each of you. You are not accountable for your mentee's duties at work, nor need to satisfy performance requirements. That allows the relationship to really breathe. In fact, you may be working on mentee aspirations that are well beyond the walls of your mentee's current job. If there are relationship obstacles between the two of you, you will need to get those resolved for the benefit of the mentoring.

You are also a role model, bringing your best self to the relationship and serving in the best interest of your mentee. What is particularly unique is the opportunity to explore mindsets, feelings, and perceptions that influence the mentee's behavior. You are helping your mentee to explore both inwardly and outwardly.

## Distinguishing From Others Who Help Mentees Grow

Let's explore the differences between your role as mentor and four important roles that also help develop your mentee.

### Manager Who Is a Coach

The manager-coach has an eye on expanding performance and company retention of the employee, with the employee (mentee) viewed as a company asset. While that manager will help with developing greater competencies and possibly career moves, it is in the context of the organization's needs, and retaining the employee. So for example, as the employee discusses career moves with their manager, they are almost always considering roles that are typically on the path of the current job. There can be an expectation that what is discussed in their meetings is not confidential, making it tough for the mentee to fully express ideas and address certain issues related to their organizational life.

### External Coach

The external coach is a paid professional on a contract, usually by the organization, and may have an overarching objective as established by the company. The external coach is highly skilled and certified in coaching methods (many of which mentors also aspire to use) and assessments. The coach will establish an enriching relationship and, like a mentor, will establish a safe zone for in-depth conversations to help the employee explore and test new behaviors. Coaches are masters of growth and development and have dedicated their professional careers to this endeavor. As an example, the talent management department may bring in an external coach to prepare a high-performing, strategically minded professional to take on a leadership role. When the coach's contract has been fulfilled, although the employee may want to continue the relationship, that relationship will likely end or significantly change focus.

## Consultant

Similar to the external coach, a consultant is a highly skilled professional on a paid contract. The consultant is typically working on a specific project or organizational change and may work closely, even one on one, with the employee. The partnership may be developmental for the employee, and they will learn a great deal. In the end, the consultant is largely focused on the larger organizational project and the related outcomes. Similar to the paid external coach, when the contract ends, the relationship will likely end or change focus.

## Trusted Colleague

With the individual's trusted colleague, a bond of trust and respect can be created. Similar to a mentor, the colleague is voluntary and "at will," and that can underlie a strong connection. With a trusted colleague, the employee can share feedback, which can be especially useful if that person sees the employee in action. These relationships are very important for development and should be nurtured. In fact, research shows that we have more satisfying and productive work lives when we have trusted friends at work (Burkus 2017). But few employees have a trusted colleague with the skills, experience, and perspective of a mentor. Colleagues do not usually set goals and a pathway for achieving certain skills development over a period of time. There is no contract in place; so when one gets busy, becomes envious, or the relationship no longer feels mutual, the ongoing conversations can dwindle or end abruptly.

• • •

All four of these relationship types are incredibly valuable for your mentee and should be cultivated and enjoyed. Yet, only you play the unique role of mentor. You can potentially change a mentee's path and even work life. Now, let's delve into the foundational principles of your role.

# Use the Seven Guiding Principles of Successful Mentors

Christina is director of a financial analytics function for a global business-to-business products company. She is also a seasoned mentor. She has repeatedly gotten rave reviews from her mentees, and in turn, her mentees have gotten stellar feedback from their managers regarding their increased capabilities. Paul, a 29-year-old who had recently gotten promoted into a senior analyst role, had been matched with Christina, and they spent a year mentoring together. Paul shared what he particularly revered in Christina: "It did not take long for me to feel exceptionally comfortable talking with Christina," Paul said, "and I looked forward to each of our meetings, making them a priority even when my calendar was jammed." He felt understood and respected, even though their worlds were not the same. She encouraged him to speak freely about his successes, concerns, and mistakes.

"In a word," Paul said, "I felt safe in our conversations." That safety allowed Paul to open up and explore both his aspirations as well as what it would take to get there. "Our conversations had both structure and flexibility. We would often brainstorm, with Christina giving me the lead in those discussions. Christina had a lot of great ideas, resources, and broad perspective on the business. We always ended our conversations with me describing next steps I would take at work to try out new approaches that would expand my skills. She was so encouraging. We discussed the steps sufficiently so that I could take actions on things I never thought I would do, such as recommending an approach to repair conditions with a troubled, large client account. It really raised my confidence about formulating an information-backed turnaround plan, asserting my educated point of view, and presenting customer strategy to upper management. I figured it was time to push myself into trying new things, and I could always come back to Christina for help and to make sense out of what happened."

Christina is clearly a talented mentor. But was she a natural from her very first mentoring experience? No, and very few mentors are. It takes a focused effort and practice. She developed her skills by learning from experts, self-reflection, and experimenting with new behaviors with each successive mentee. Though she had always been comfortable with in-depth conversations, she still hit roadblocks and surprises, and discovered a great deal about herself in the process. What she learned through mentoring actually ended up changing how she managed and developed her team at work, and also positively affected how she interacted at home and with friends.

As you think about yourself in the role as mentor, consider the seven guiding principles in Figure 1-1, and see if you can pick out where they resonate in Paul's description of Christina. Much more about these guiding principles will unfold in the upcoming chapters.

## FIGURE 1-1
### THE SEVEN GUIDING PRINCIPLES OF SUCCESSFUL MENTORS

## 1. Start Where Your Mentee Is (Not Where You Think They Should Be)

At times, mentors have different hopes for their mentees than mentees have for themselves. Understand that your mentee's aspirations and goals represent their best thinking at that time and are important to them. So, get a good fix on your own assumptions about what would be best, and hold that off to the side. Learn more about bringing out their best and making them a success, even if it looks nothing like what you had in mind.

Here's an example from a father-daughter conversation that can easily be applied to mentoring. In a restaurant at the table next to mine, I overheard a teenager joyfully tell her dad, "I know what I'd like to major in at college. I would love to be a sixth-grade teacher." Her dad responded, "Well OK, but not sure that's really a good choice; you'll have low pay. Maybe you should think about a marketing degree instead." Tears formed in his daughter's eyes. This example brings home the point that being driven by your own interests about what will be good for your mentee leads to disconnects, withholding thoughts, and stalled progress, because they will be working on (or fighting with) your agenda, not their own. Once you join on their playing field and they feel trusted and respected, you will be in a better place to have them consider your ideas. Honor who they are; this process is personally tailored, not prescriptive. Other mentors who have put this to use report that being guided by this principle actually leads to more satisfying results for both the mentor and the mentee.

## 2. Create a Conversational Safety Space

A conversational safety space is created when your mentee feels trusted, respected, and understood. In this space, you encourage the mentee to fully express themselves without judgment. This requires the mentor to demonstrate both self-awareness and discipline. Experienced mentors go well beyond listening for content, tuning into the mentee's attitudes and feelings. This type of conversation is the hallmark for successful mentoring. Because the mentee knows the discussion is confidential, they can share what they may not share elsewhere, so new avenues can be explored, assumptions examined, and approaches discussed. Without safety, your mentee will hold back or give you answers they think you want to hear.

**POINTER**

Without safety, your mentee will hold back or give you answers they think you want to hear.

## 3. Cultivate a Positive and Resilient Relationship

The quality of the relationship is the primary tool for the mentoring process. Acceptance, mutual respect, and transparency are all part of that, and important for you to model. Though you are both participants in the relationship, you have the lead in observing how the relationship is going and taking steps to ensure its vitality. A real test comes when there are differences, and you do not like their approach or attitude, or they yours. Yet, building the relationship from that point forward is required, and your mentee will need to do the same. It shows that relationships can be strong, even if ideas are not totally aligned. A positive environment is where new ideas, creativity, and insight flourish. Welcome the unexpected; when anger or frustration does arise, use these to explore a constructive outcome.

## 4. Be Flexibly Goal Oriented

Your work together requires a jointly understood goal for development. Without a goal, you may drift around and find interesting things to talk about, but accomplishments will be limited. Make the most of your time, and deliver real results—big results. The goal is set early in your process, based on thoughtful consideration. As the mentor, be attuned during each meeting to reach for the relevance of that conversation toward accomplishing the goal. At the same time, your conversations should not feel like a project team meeting that is in constant press to get tasks accomplished. Allow for off-the-path exploration, and leave open the possibilities for surprises. Revisit the goal periodically for the possibility of modifying the goal based on the mentee's latest circumstances.

## 5. Drive Risk Taking for New Mindsets and Behaviors

A paradoxical action is that you provide safety in the mentoring relationship, only to then push your mentee to take risks. Yet, it is the very safety of you being in the wings that allows your mentee to boldly take new and uncomfortable behaviors. In the case of Christina and Paul, he took a significant leap—not little progressive steps, in proposing a solution and then leading the charge. Leading up to this, Christina took the position of being both supportive and tough. There will be little growth if your mentee only thinks or talks about new actions and behaviors; your mentee actually has to try those on for size. Aim high. Have your mentee stretch outside their comfort zone on a continuous basis, and help them view mishaps as part of the learning process that will be debriefed and then perfected for the next actions. This requires resilience on their part and yours.

**POINTER**

The paradoxical nature to mentoring is that you provide safety in the relationship, only to then push your mentee to take risks.

## 6. Explore the Internal World as a Driver for External Actions

Your mentee's effectiveness is greatly shaped by their self-awareness. How well they can tune in to understand their own motives, preferences, strengths, and weaknesses will help determine the quality of interactions with others. By creating the conversational safety space, you are in a great spot to use productive questions and have them explore what prompts them, bringing the hidden drivers of behavior into consciousness. You can help them check out assumptions, perspectives, fears, and impact on others, all aimed toward more effective interactions. This book has dedicated an entire chapter to this important element of mentoring (Step 6: The Power of Questions), helping you to open new pathways of insight for your mentee.

## 7. Bring Your Best Self

It is amazing just how much influence a mentor has with a mentee. As a mentor, you are studied for your attitudes, your work habits, how you handle mishaps, your professionalism, and more. It is a big responsibility to be someone's admired role model. Be fully present and prepared for each meeting, and manage the interactions with your mentee for the best possible outcomes. You are not expected to be a superhero, just a really great mentor. Continue to develop yourself while you are helping to develop your mentee. And, while you are at it, consider what it means to be inspirational. You will continue to be a marvelous mentor.

# Review the Seven Guiding Principles

Consider how you are experiencing these seven guiding principles of successful mentors. These are core to the work you will be doing as a mentor. Pause for a bit and consider these questions: How are these making you feel? What excites you? What intrigues you? What scares you?

These seven guiding principles are not merely present at one time or another in your mentoring; these seven are present for each and every meeting! The good news is that you will hardly be starting from scratch. You already have many of the skills that are crucial elements of these principles, such as listening, being open to other perspectives, compassion, self-insight, and tenaciously following through for results. Capitalize on these and the many other skills you already have. As you apply these principles, pay attention to the skills you will need to enrich; learning is an important aspect of your own journey as mentor. Mastering these guiding principles will be as enlightening as it is gratifying. Frequently check in with Tool 1-1 to keep these top of mind.

## TOOL 1-1

### THE ESSENTIALS OF THE SEVEN GUIDING PRINCIPLES OF SUCCESSFUL MENTORS

| Guiding Principle | What Is Required of You |
|---|---|
| 1. Start where your mentee is. | • Ask questions to understand your mentee's aspirations.<br>• Listen to your mentee's interests and probe for even more.<br>• Be mindful of your assumptions about your mentee's needs and set those aside. |

STEP 1

| Guiding Principle | What Is Required of You |
|---|---|
| 2. Create a conversational safety space. | • Show confidence in and respect for your mentee. <br> • Strengthen trust through your actions, which in turn will build reliability, credibility, and candor. <br> • Ensure your conversations are private and confidential. |
| 3. Cultivate a positive and resilient relationship. | • Observe what is going on in the dynamics of your relationship. <br> • Initiate check-ins to discuss how your process is going. <br> • Welcome feedback from your mentee and offer yours. |
| 4. Be flexibly goal oriented. | • Be deliberate about your mentee's development by having a well-crafted goal(s). <br> • Reconnect to the mentee's development goals during every meeting. <br> • Invite discovery through "off-the-path" excursions. |
| 5. Drive risk taking for new mindsets and behaviors. | • Push your mentee to tolerate, even enjoy, being uncomfortable. <br> • Support your mentee to put new mindsets and behaviors into real-time action. <br> • Use mishaps as a key element of the development process. |
| 6. Explore the internal world as the driver for external actions. | • Understand and apply the basics of everyday psychology and neuroscience. <br> • Use productive questioning to help your mentee uncover motivations, assumptions, and other internal drivers of behavior. <br> • Help create your mentee's habit of reflection, especially after key interactions. |
| 7. Bring your best self. | • Prepare for and be fully present at each meeting. <br> • Take actions worthy of "admired role model" status. <br> • Continue with your own development while supporting your mentee's growth. |

## Understand Your Motivation for Being a Mentor

When asked what got her started as a mentor, Christina stated a five-word response provided by thousands of other mentors: "I wanted to give back." She continued, "I had come to a point in my own life where I had achieved a lot of career satisfaction and then wondered what was next for me. And, I decided it was time to share what I had to offer. It took me a little while to wrap my head around how this would be different from the way I manage and develop my team members at work, and what I really hoped to get out of it. I wanted it to be distinct from what I had in other relationships and wanted to do it right. Once I was clear about that, I felt very, very driven to do this."

In your own preparation to be a mentor, exploring your hopes and motivations will identify what you are bringing to this mentoring (something you can share with your mentee later), your underlying assumptions, and the preferences you have about mentoring.

Your attraction to being a mentor likely emanates from a number of experiences and personal characteristics. Perhaps you had a mentor who left a significant impression by helping you in pivotal moments of your life, or you lacked a mentor and can relate to the feeling of isolation in handling challenges on your own. You may naturally enjoy nurturing others, have an affinity for social responsibility, or want to contribute to your field. Whatever your spark, you are now finding great satisfaction in helping another, and creating a bridge to someone's successful future based on your own experiences, knowledge, and wisdom.

The timing to become a mentor is no coincidence. It is actually human nature to have this interest once we have created a full life and experience success in our careers. Well-known psychologist Erik Erikson identified that as adults, after we have mastered shaping our identity and forming lasting relationships, we move into a desire for "generativity," crafting a legacy by creating or nurturing things that will live on past our careers and lives. Having mentees, and benefitting their lives, is one of the ways to fulfill our need to leave our mark and be part of something bigger than our

## POINTER

Helping to make a positive and productive impact on another's life is a complex effort. Tuning into your motivation, assumptions, and expectations will help to clarify your current starting point.

own world. It is a way we feel more complete and satisfies our own needs to be whole (McLeod 2018).

Helping to make a positive and productive impact on another's life is a complex effort. Each person who is drawn to mentor carries their distinctive view of what mentoring is all about. From this book, you will learn more deeply what it means to mentor an adult for their professional development. Whether you mentor someone younger than yourself or someone your own age or older who seeks your help in their development, the seven guiding principles of mentors already give you ideas about what will be most important. Tuning into your motivation, assumptions, and expectations will help to clarify your current starting point, an important part of your preparation. If ideas you encounter in the book are different from your own, if there are surprises, it will be worth you time to consider how to shape the best path forward. Tool 1-2 is an exercise for you, similar to what Christina did, to be fully prepared for mentoring. Think through the following questions to uncover your motivation and assumptions.

## TOOL 1-2
### QUESTIONS TO UNCOVER YOUR MOTIVATION AND ASSUMPTIONS ABOUT MENTORING

1. What does being a mentor mean to me?
2. What skills, mindsets, and approaches am I bringing to this role?
3. What are my assumptions about best approaches to use in mentoring?
4. What do I want from the mentoring relationship?
5. How will mentoring be different from other roles I play (e.g., parent, friend, manager)?
6. How will I manage my expectations of the ideal mentoring experience (that I carry in my head)?
7. How will I know that the mentoring has been successful?
8. What do I hope to learn during this mentoring experience?

# Participate in a Program or Create Your Own

From the initial introduction to your mentee through to the wrap-up of the mentoring, there are deliberate steps that make the journey highly valuable and memorable. When you know what to expect in the phases of your work together, there is a true sense of a journey to a destination, rather than wandering around or having a new target for each meeting. A framework strengthens the partnership and keeps your actions moving forward. It works just as well and is equally important, whether you are part of a formal mentoring program or not. If you are not working in the setting of an organized program, create a framework for the mentoring that can be shared with your mentee.

The length of your program can vary and is somewhat determined by how often you meet. Meeting frequency is either once or twice a month, for 60-90 minutes. In company programs, because an objective is to include new mentees regularly, the duration is typically six to 12 months in length, with an informal option to meet on a less frequent basis afterward. In such company programs, the pairs might meet 10-15 times over the course of mentoring, and a tremendous amount of development can occur in that time. For those of you mentoring independent of a program, the length can be longer than a year, and it is advised that you check in at least quarterly to identify an approximate completion date. Identifying when you will wrap up, and not leaving it open ended, allows you to put into motion the vital closure steps, crucial to the lasting impact of the mentoring process (see step 10 for more details).

Tool 1-3 is a sample framework for your ongoing mentoring, whether you are in a formal program or on your own. Notice it has distinct focus for the first few meetings and the last few meetings. In the middle is the ongoing work of deepening your relationship to support the mentee's quest to expand, develop, and field-test new behaviors and mindsets. Through this process the mentee will work through old assumptions and perspectives, experiment with new ways of behaving, feel more confident, and experience the potential for increased impact. In the end, mentees will be improved versions of themselves . . . and you will be as well.

# TOOL 1-3

# THE MENTORING PROCESS FRAMEWORK

STEP 1

| Phase | Timeframe | Mentor's Focus |
|---|---|---|
| Establishing the relationship | First 2 meetings | • Get to know one another; find common ground.<br>• Set the tone for the quality of your conversations.<br>• Guide a discussion about your roles and expectations. |
| Setting the direction | First 3-4 meetings | • Explore mentee's aspirations.<br>• Guide mentee to set meaningful and actionable development goals.<br>• Establish a method for your meetings.<br>• Identify how momentum for development will occur between meetings. |
| Exploring your mentee's current work experiences and applying new mindsets and behaviors | Ongoing meetings | • Explore mentee's day-to-day experiences and interactions.<br>• Leverage work experiences as prime avenue for development.<br>• Ensure your relationship is healthy and address obstacles.<br>• Jointly monitor progress of goals accomplishment; adjust as needed.<br>• Elevate the power of questions to raise insights.<br>• Inspire confidence and hope.<br>• Help mentee increase self-awareness and broaden perspectives.<br>• Encourage mentee to experiment with new behaviors.<br>• Track own progress, speak with other mentors, and deepen your skill set. |
| Perfecting your mentee's new capabilities | Last third of meetings | • Diversify approaches to mentee's development.<br>• Encourage mentee's taking risks by applying expanded skill sets in new settings.<br>• Increase mentee's influence skills to provide a larger platform for applying enhanced capabilities.<br>• Urge mentee to take a more pivotal role where new skills can be applied. |

| Phase | Timeframe | Mentor's Focus |
|---|---|---|
| Anticipating closure and wrapping up | Last 2-3 meetings | • Identify priority areas for further discussion in last couple meetings.<br>• Jointly establish an end date.<br>• Prime the mentee for the value and content of the wrap-up conversation.<br>• Facilitate a meaningful and positive wrap-up conversation.<br>• Consolidate your own learning, especially with other mentors. |

# Consider the Readiness Checklist

Tool 1-4 presents a readiness checklist for the work ahead. Some of the items will intrigue you and others will be a piece of cake. Remember that you will be supported in this book to do all of the following.

## TOOL 1-4
### MENTORING READINESS CHECKLIST

Get ready to . . .

❑ Learn about the program you are part of and resources you can turn to.

❑ Commit the time it takes for a steady, ongoing relationship.

❑ Consider your motivations, preferences, strengths, and expectations as a mentor.

❑ Facilitate early discussions with your mentee focused on developing the relationship.

❑ Identify where you would like to grow as a mentor.

❑ Help mentee set important goals and establish a mentoring game plan.

❑ Ask productive questions and listen to connect.

❑ Tune up your flexibility and be prepared for surprises.

❑ Share the experience with other mentors for support and enrichment.

❑ Help mentee become more self-aware and create a habit of reflecting on interactions.

❑ Maintain a positive attitude and outlook in the face of challenges.

STEP 1

- ❑ Encourage your mentee to set up fieldwork and experiments to test new mindsets and behaviors.
- ❑ Diversify approaches to your mentee's development.
- ❑ Push mentee to up their skill set, influence others, and accomplish bigger results.
- ❑ Facilitate the wrap-up and closure to mentoring.
- ❑ Have a gratifying, growth-producing experience for yourself.

# The Next Step

The next crucial step in the mentoring process is establishing the relationship. During this step, you will explore how you and your mentee will get to know each other, create a trusting and respectful partnership, clarify expectations, and reach mutual agreement about what you will be carrying out in this mentoring alliance. This will create a strong foundation for the myriad actions you will take together over the months ahead, resulting in career-changing growth.

# Step 2

# Establish the Relationship

*"I am not what you see. I am what time and effort and interaction slowly unveil."*

*–Richelle E. Goodrich*

## Overview

- Gain an understanding of your partner.
- Find common ground.
- Clarify expectations of working together.
- Identify your roles.
- Create a mutual agreement.

"Have to admit, I am surprised at how nervous I feel about my first conversation with Jessica. How do I make sure things are started right? It feels like I'm in a spotlight." This is what Kal, an accomplished manager who was becoming a first-time mentor, shared with me. His mentee, a fast-rising professional in his field, was someone he had never met; they had been paired through the company's mentoring program. Kal had a compelling desire to be a masterful mentor, yet was keenly aware of his limited experience. (This is much better than Kal saying he had read a book on mentoring, had a firm plan, and knew every move he'd take.)

Should Kal be so concerned? After all, we meet new people all the time. Yet, not quite like this. At the start of most relationships, we're meeting someone because we are obligated to work with them, such as a boss or co-worker—or, if in a social context, we can proceed or not, depending how we feel about that person. In the case of new mentoring, we anticipate a high investment; one that is voluntary, and developing a bond to work together sight unseen. The value in getting this startup right is that it will allow the two of you to move more quickly into the work, helping the mentee share ideas and concerns, increase confidence, and widen perspective.

At the start, the responsibility to establish the relationship rests more on your shoulders than your mentee's. During your first meeting, aim to cover the items that will make you each feel comfortable to move forward; no need to discuss everything under the sun. This chapter will show you what is the important ground to cover . . . and that starts with how you enter the conversation, and understanding the interests and ambitions of your mentee.

## Gain an Understanding of Your Partner

Even before you ever have a word of conversation, the relationship can get jump-started by the exchange of resumes or bios, and an online check of each other's background through social media. As a bonus, if there was an application process for the mentoring program that asks why you want to participate and what you hope to get out of the program, you can each review this material to open doors toward setting mutual expectations.

**POINTER**

When leading the first discussion to learn about each other, it is equally important to consider how you approach the conversation as much as it is what you ask about.

When leading the first discussion to learn about each other, it is equally important to consider *how* you approach the conversation as much as it is what you ask about. Since a first impression is lasting, an effective "how" shows your intention to be authentic and sincerely curious about the mentee.

## Prepare for the "How" of Your First Conversation

How will you present yourself to your mentee during that first meeting? Get ready by doing a quick check to determine your state of mind. Some mentors, for example, are eager to prove their substantial level of expertise, or perhaps show their nurturing side. While that's only natural, during this conversation, make the mentee the star. With antennae up, your mentee will pick up nonverbal cues quicker than verbal ones, scanning for likability and respect. And, consider that your mentee, too, comes to the conversations with a particular state of mind (for example, wanting to be the best darned mentee anyone has ever seen, or, conversely, feeling overwhelmed by meeting the great and powerful you).

Here is an example with learning that came from hindsight. Near the end of the six-month mentoring relationship, Leah found out from her mentee, Jonas, that when they started their work together, Jonas was quite apprehensive. After he had looked up her profile online, he came into that first meeting viewing Leah as a hot shot; and during that first meeting, Leah's commanding tone and reference to her many career successes only reinforced his trepidation. So Jonas held back, feeling he did not measure up. It took him a couple months until he felt safe enough to reveal his weaker sides, areas where he wasn't doing so well at work. Leah was utterly unaware of this! Too bad for Leah and Jonas; with only a six-month duration in this program, they lost precious time at the front end. Leah learned a big lesson and took it to heart in subsequent first meetings with mentees: It is far more important to be impressed by your mentee than to be impressive yourself (mentors already cast a big shadow).

Preparation before this conversation should also have you thinking about some potential biases. Yes, we can all have some biases, and it is better to be aware rather than let them send us off course. There are particularly two types that can pop up.

First is one I call the "preferred mentee profile" bias. This bias became crystal clear when Henry, a mentor in a program I manage, gave me a check list of attributes he hoped would be found in the mentee with whom he was to be matched (for example, exceptionally bright, proven track record of growth in the company, diligent, great interpersonal skills). "Yeah, Henry," I thought to myself, "all the mentors want that person." Then I wondered: Suppose he was matched with a mentee who did not fulfill his list; would he look at them with disappointment? Would he be as good a mentor to someone who did not fit his preferred profile? As with any mentor, to establish a well-grounded relationship, Henry would need to be aware of his bias, steer clear of any judgments, and embrace the qualities and background of his mentee.

The second bias is the "summed up before I meet you" bias. This bias is built on assumptions mentors make from reading the mentee's resume or hearing about the mentee from others, painting a mental portrait that may or may not be completely true. Examining your unconscious biases requires you to pause after you learn about your mentee and identify where you might slide into making assumptions, based on what was triggered in you about your mentee's background (for example, education was in a different field than career, worked for a competing company, had a series of jobs with less than a year's tenure). Doing this will help you to learn more about yourself and be more effective during your first mentee meeting.

## Prepare for the "What" of Your First Conversation

AJ, a seasoned mentor, is both thoughtful and easygoing about his approach to the initial meeting with his mentees. He makes the "what" a combination of personal and professional questions with suitable boundaries for a first-time meeting. He says that mentees want to show up well, and it is very appropriate for them to hold off sharing deeper challenges for a later conversation. A revealing opener he uses is to have his mentee and him ask each other these two questions: "What brought you into the mentoring program?" and "What do you hope to learn through your involvement in this mentoring?" He allows the conversation to flow from there.

Similar to AJ's approach, allowing for flexibility in the discussion will point you toward what is important for the mentee. For example, a mentee might speak of the most gratifying parts of a job, work environment, or desire for greater responsibility. As the conversation unwinds, it can be easy to start covering all manner of subjects. At the same time, take on the role of pacing the discussion. Be sure to cover the basics, gently steering the conversation to ensure that by the end the meeting the expected outcomes of the conversation are reached. It is excessive to gather all the background information in this first discussion; hold some delights and surprises for later.

Consider Tool 2-1 as a thoughtful and focused version of a dual interview with a number of preset questions that you and your mentee can ask.

## Tool 2-1
### Sample Questions to Gain an Understanding of Your Mentoring Partner

- What brought you into the mentoring program?
- Mentor asks mentee:
    - What has been important in your (career) development to this point?
    - What is going on in your work life right now?
    - What are your aspirations?
    - Where is your career headed?
- Mentee asks mentor:
    - What have been significant events that have shaped your career?
    - What are you doing currently that is most engaging?
    - What kinds of things at work and elsewhere bring you joy?
- What stood out to you from previous mentoring you have been involved with?
- What would you like to learn during this mentoring process?
- What do you hope will be different for you at the end of this program?
- What is a personal strength you bring to the mentoring relationship?

# Find Common Ground

A TV reality series, first begun in Denmark in 2014 and immediately franchised into a half-dozen other countries, can give us a window into the early meeting of mentor and mentee. In the TV program "Married at First Sight," couples complete detailed applications, and professionals (psychologists and others) work to match the pairs, based upon backgrounds, lifestyles, choices, and more. The couples first meet each other at their wedding! The show is oddly captivating, based around the idea that no matter if your matched spouse meets your expectations or not, each individual has committed to make it work for an eight-week period. The couples are supported throughout the process, given lots of tips and coaching, yet make their own choices—nothing is forced. Viewers watch as each new spouse sizes up their partner, looks for attributes they like, and asks questions of each other. Mostly, it seems, they are initially searching for similarities or desirable attributes. Shortly after the wedding, they talk about what they like about each other, the surprises, and the attributes that are different than expected.

Though mentors and mentees are hardly taking this kind of huge lifetime leap, many mentors are in a mentoring program with matches created for them by a program manager, with the best of intentions. So a mentor might wonder, "Now that I signed up to mentor, will I like that person? Will she like me? Will this be worth my (discretionary) time and effort?" In that first meeting, you search for common ground and characteristics that meet your expectations. There is an eagerness to learn a lot about each other, most especially to find commonalities, which is a good place to get started. Commonalities create a feeling of acceptability and safety.

In a research article in *Harvard Business Review,* David DeSteno (2016) shares that when building relationships, a powerful tool is a sense of similarity, that people's interests are joined and therefore, they are on the same team. The truth is that if we really look, we can find commonalities with anyone, because we all share the human

experience. Even if your upbringing, education, and career are different, if you search, you will find where you overlap. Whether it is
growing up in a small town, enjoying a certain sport, even caring for
an ailing family member, taking note of that creates a connection.
Underscore those commonalities in your conversation; it creates a
comfort, and a basis for the bond. For example, you may find you
have common ground with some of these:

STEP **2**

- favorite college experience or courses
- early work experiences
- challenges with boss or colleagues
- preferred work habits
- memorable team events.

With over 16 years of participating in or managing a mentoring
program, I have been fortunate to watch scores of mentoring pairs
meet for the first time. For many pairs, at the front end, there is a
sort of euphoria, believing they have found their
true match. Others may politely hide disappointment as their partner is not who they expected. As
a mentor myself, I have had it both ways, so I hold
my emotions in check. Reading the mentee's resume
and application to the program, I used to conjure
up all types of images—how they are similar to me,
what their interests are, where I think they are headed
career-wise, or how they are so different. And guess
what? What I imagined at first panned out to be
correct less than half the time.

Mentors and mentees are each looking for alignment of values to establish mutual respect and gain
trust. They want the other to value what they bring
to the relationship, which stems from their person-
al history: choices made at crucial life junctures, risks taken, special
interests, and growth they have made. Mutual respect takes shape
when they listen attentively, learn about what is important to the
other, and honor that.

**POINTER**

Mentors and
mentees are each
looking for align-
ment of values to
establish mutual
respect and gain
trust. Mutual
respect takes
shape when they
listen attentively,
learn about what
is important to the
other, and honor
that.

For example, Jacob was having his first discussion with his new mentee, Raisha, using a handful of preset questions. When he asked Raisha about role models, she told Jacob that the most important lessons came from her aunt, who was wheelchair bound. Jacob felt her emotion as she spoke. Rather than simply take note of this and then move on to the next question, he took time to make several inquiries about those lessons, how the lessons shaped her decisions, and how she and her aunt related to each other. He thanked her for sharing those stories and told her how powerful they were. Raisha later told him that his questions and exploration about her aunt touched her and she immediately felt very respected by him. At that moment, the caution she carried into that first meeting melted away.

Of course, there will be differences between you and your mentees as well, and these differences will be an excellent source for relationship building. In this early stage, acknowledge these with anticipation as a place for learning from each other's perspectives. Respecting differences is the stuff trust is made of.

## Clarify Expectations of Working Together

The relationship you are building will be one of a kind. Unlike in the workplace, there are fewer rules and more freedom to establish how you will work together. Within the structure of your mentoring program, mutually setting the framework tailors it to both of your styles. How will you work together to accomplish great results? What are the best ways to communicate? How will you handle disconnects? All are the right questions to ask and deserve your attention. These all move you in the direction of Guiding Principle #3: Cultivate a positive and resilient relationship. Making assumptions or believing your past successful experiences determine the best path forward may undermine a collaborative and meaningful connection. Identify what works for each of you, and what could get in the way. Asking about whether to use office, home, or cell phone won't take much effort, and will be a timesaver. Be responsive and realistic; avoid over promising, but be willing to stretch.

Use a list of items, like the one in Tool 2-2, to clarify your expectations. Later, turn this conversation into a documented mutual agreement about how you will be working together.

## TOOL 2-2
### SEVEN TOPICS TO DISCUSS ABOUT WORKING TOGETHER

| Topics About Working Together | Consider These Questions |
|---|---|
| 1. Overall objectives | What is the purpose of this mentoring? What will constitute success for each of us? |
| 2. Use of a mentee development plan | How will we use the mentee development plan to target specific goals, guide our forward progress, and periodically check on progress against the goals? |
| 3. Preferred ways to communicate | What is the preferred way to communicate in between meetings (e.g., emails, phone call at office or on mobile, video calls, texts)? |
| 4. Meetings and scheduling | How often, when, and where will we be meeting? What will be the length of our meetings? How we will handle the need to reschedule? What will be the length of this working relationship (e.g., a set five months or open ended and to be revisited regularly after the six-month marker?) |
| 5. Scope of discussion content | What will be our primary subject matter (e.g., work related successes and challenges, developing specific skills, career opportunities)? What is off the table (e.g., life choices, purchasing a home, finances)? |
| 6. Safety and confidentiality | How will we handle sensitive topics? What does "confidential" mean for each of us? |
| 7. Providing feedback | How can we ensure regular check-ins with each other on how it is going? How will we discuss the aspects of mentoring that are not working well? What might get in the way, and how do we want to address those obstacles? |

# Identify Your Roles

Seasoned mentors avoid coming into the effort believing they know what's required in this new relationship. Consider that mentoring programs are created to serve a multitude of potential purposes such as career advancement, leader development, retention, and specific skill development. And, as the purpose of the program can vary, so do the requirements of the mentor. Let's take a look at the mentor and mentee roles in turn, focusing on the responsibilities and behaviors.

## Mentor Responsibilities and Behaviors

If your work as a mentor is part of a larger program, the program will likely spell out your responsibilities. These stated mentor responsibilities can be readily shared with your mentee, as both a hard-copy handout and verbally. If your mentoring is separate from any program, it is essential to be clear about how you view your role and convey that to your mentee. Since a significant aspect of building and maintaining trust is reliability, consistently delivering on your role, as defined in a handout you provide to your mentee, will be important. Your mentoring then becomes more predictable, and the collaboration more secure. Over time the mentee can return to the document if accountabilities in the relationship are unclear; it empowers the mentee to raise questions if the routine changes (for example, when a mentor unilaterally changes the pattern of their meetings).

Here is a sample of mentor responsibilities from the Philadelphia Society for People and Strategy's professional development mentoring program, which I helped to manage for a decade:

- Participate in all mentoring program meetings: kickoff, midpoint check in, and wrap-up conducted via webinar.
- Conduct early conversations about how you will operate as a mentoring partnership, what the mentee's development goal for the mentorship is, how you will handle providing each other feedback.
- Meet twice monthly with mentee for 60 to 90 minutes, at a time that works for both of you.

- Focus on professional growth (versus "life" challenges).
- Use a coaching approach: ask questions, focus on the mentee's experiences and how they can be used to grow capabilities, avoid solving problems for the mentee.
- Help the mentee track progress and drive completion of set development goals.
- Apply "boundary management" (that is, maintaining confidentiality, keeping the association professional) so that a trusting relationship is built without overdependency.
- Push the envelope; drive for a real stretch for both mentee and yourself.
- Provide resources such as articles, TED Talks, and those who can be resources for conversations on specific capabilities.
- Demonstrate commitment to the process, advocate for and support your mentee.
- Take the lead in the mentoring process wrap-up.

A powerful aspect of the role is mentor behaviors. This is where your true mentor mastery comes in. As good at this as you are today, you'll always want to be better. Developing the most effective behaviors requires both learning new as well as breaking old habits. Take a look at Figure 2-1, which identifies the six behaviors that will be important in your work ahead.

## FIGURE 2-1

## SIX MENTOR BEHAVIORS CRUCIAL FOR MENTOR MASTERY

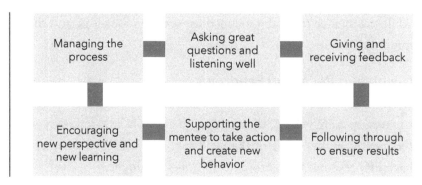

In today's environment, the mentor serves as a coach, facilitator, questioner, resource provider, and more. Your behaviors should spur the mentee's thinking and problem solving, widen their perspective, encourage them to take new steps, raise their confidence, and provide food for thought. Thinking about your role as guru, teacher, and problem solver is old school. As a seasoned mentor, AJ offers this advice to his new mentor colleagues: "Though tempting to do, mentoring is not about giving them the solution to the problems they face; it is about helping them figure out the best way to solve it for themselves, with you in the wings cheering them on." This is all in service of Guiding Principle #7: Bring your best self. In carrying out your role, here are some tips on how you can embody the six behaviors that promote learning and collaboration with your mentee:

## Managing the Process

Track progress both in the mentoring relationship and toward mentees' development goals. Ensure meetings occur with regularity and are meaningful. Provide safety by being accepting and judgment free. Allow for mistakes (be tolerant and patient) and turn those into learning experiences.

## Asking Great Questions and Listening Well

Ask questions that encourage the mentee to increase self-awareness, consider the context of the situation they are encountering, and explore possible solutions. Allow for silence, giving open space while the mentee talks about concerns, searches for ideas, and shares important stories.

## Giving and Receiving Feedback

Assess readiness of mentee to receive and use feedback. Be courageous to caringly share what you see in your mentee's behavior. Listen while the mentee makes sense of the feedback. Ask for the mentee's feedback and respond to it. Promote an honest dialogue.

### Encouraging New Perspective and New Learning

Challenge the mentee to see beyond their role and immediate dilemma. Help them view the situation or tasks from the vantage point of others, and ask them to talk with trusted colleagues about it. Spur the mentee to increase knowledge and skills to better understand and work with the world around them.

### Supporting the Mentee to Take Action and Create New Behaviors

Explore different actions that can deliver an improved or bigger result. Prepare the mentee to test new approaches at work. Debrief after new actions are tried to discuss impact and help fine-tune the actions.

### Following Through to Assure Results

Deliver on promises you made for providing information, resources, or to discuss specific topics. Offer ongoing support of new actions the mentee has taken and mine the learning from those. Give your mentee confidence to address persistent difficulties at work. Identify and encourage next steps.

STEP 2

• • •

As you describe the role expectations, invite your mentee to ask any questions. That way, the two-way dialogue secures a shared understanding. There is a lot more to come on all of these mentor behaviors as you continue reading this book.

## Mentee Responsibilities and Behaviors

This is a mutual relationship. While you take a lead role in overseeing the process, much of the work toward accomplishing results happens with the mentee; they cannot be passive. Established mentoring programs set criteria for mentee selection, and screening is done to ensure the mentee is ready. Then, mentees start off with a briefing which includes familiarity with their responsibilities. If these elements are not present for your mentoring, prepare for the initial meeting by having suggestions in hand.

Start the conversation about mentee responsibilities by asking your mentee what they believe is most important in their role. Your question-and-answer dialogue will clarify how they define and view these accountabilities. From there you can pose additional role elements, if needed. Here are some sample mentee responsibilities you can both draw from:

- Participate fully in meetings: kick-off, midpoint check-in, and twice monthly with mentor, and virtual program wrap-up.
- Set clear and realistic goals, and track progress throughout the process.
- Focus on your real work and challenges, not academic questions.
- Stretch and challenge yourself, seeing things differently and trying new behaviors.
- Be accountable to work through problems and challenges in a new way.
- Gain deeper self-awareness.
- Intentionally support the process so that it works well for your mentor.
- Regularly reflect on new behaviors you are developing.

There is no question that this is a unique relationship for mentees, especially if this is their first mentoring experience. Different from the work environment, they do not have performance requirements attached to their efforts. During your work together, the mentee will benefit by being more open, reflective, and daring in trying new approaches. In the case of Jacob and Raisha, Raisha was a bit confused about the need to identify specific behaviors in the mentoring relationship, since they had just discussed her mentee responsibilities. Here's how Jacob explained it to Raisha: "Being conscious of specific behaviors to use

**POINTER**

While you take a lead role in overseeing the process, much of the work toward accomplishing results happens with the mentee; they cannot be passive.

in mentoring will make your approach to mentoring more intentional and separate it from the typical things you do at work or home. For example, learning to regularly experiment with new approaches is something you told me you do not do much of at work. If we call that out as a behavior you will use in this mentoring process, you will turn that into a developmental habit for yourself. We do not need a long list of behaviors, just several that will be most helpful to keep top of mind."

Similar to Jacob, you, too, can have such a discussion with your mentee about which behaviors will tailor to your mentee's development game plan. Here are a few mentee behaviors the two of you can consider in this early part of your relationship. Find the best fit to suit your mentee and their personality, skill set, and direction.

- Expand your perspective.
- Experiment with new behaviors.
- Lean in, even when the work gets uncomfortable.
- Respect the mentor's role and avoid boundary breaks (for example, asking for advice outside your agreed scope).
- Provide and receive feedback thoughtfully.
- Ask high-gain questions.
- Demonstrate courage and risk taking.
- Regard missteps as lessons.

Just as with the discussion about your mentor role, gain clarity, identify examples, and invite questions so the two of you have greater alignment. It won't be complete, yet far better than taking for granted you are both on the same page. Of course, the proof of your aligned view about roles will be seen in the upcoming weeks and months to come as you each move into action. Relationships evolve over time. As an example, Jacob always anticipates that he and his mentee will revisit parts of this discussion over the first few meetings, so that they can serve each other in the best ways possible.

## Create a Mutual Agreement

Now that you have covered your expectations of working together and your roles, create a mutual agreement. Some pairs use a standard form, others create their own; it is your choice. This written agreement validates your commitment to the process. More details, including the mentee development plan, may be added after a couple more meetings. Revisit this agreement; it serves as a great tool to track how you are doing, and it may be worth making modifications to it as needed (for example, when one of you has relocated, or if your mentee starts a new job). On the next page, you'll find Tool 2-3, which offers a mutual mentoring agreement template you could use.

## The Next Step

While you have created a foundation for your mentoring relationship by getting to know each other, discussing your expectations and roles, and establishing a mutual agreement, there is another vital step to lay groundwork for your mentee's memorable growth. With step 3 (Set the Direction), you will focus on formulating development goals for the mentoring process; establishing your jointly agreed-upon approach to ongoing meetings; and identifying that, importantly, your mentee will be making forward progress between your meetings.

# TOOL 2-3
## MUTUAL MENTORING AGREEMENT TEMPLATE

We identified the following expectations and role responsibilities as part of our agreement to work together in this mentoring relationship.

Overall objectives

Use of development plan

Preferred ways to communicate

Meetings, scheduling, and anticipated length of mentoring relationship

Scope of discussion content

Safety and confidentiality

Providing feedback

Mentee's responsibilities and targeted behaviors include:

Mentor's responsibilities and targeted behaviors include:

Additional considerations we have discussed:

If the mentoring relationship is assessed to not be working well, by either one of us, we agree to take steps to improve the relationship, including reaching out to a third party for counsel.

Mentee's signature _____

Date:_____

Mentor's signature _____

Date:_____

# Step 3
# **Set the Direction**

*"Efforts and courage are not enough without purpose and direction."*

*–John F. Kennedy*

## Overview

- Formulate development goals for mentoring.
- Craft a method for your meetings.
- Establish the expectation of momentum between meetings.

Not too long ago, I worked for a large company whose offices were in several buildings, connected via pass-throughs, but only on certain floors. During my initial visit to this company, after my first appointment, I called my next client to ask for directions to his office. Before he gave me an answer, what did he want to know? He wanted to know *from where I was starting.* If he just told me he was on the fifth floor, I might have wandered for quite a while, minimizing our time together, not realizing it was the fifth floor in the adjacent building, needing to cross over on floor four. Complicated. Without specific navigation, the early stage of mentoring work could similarly end up going off in the wrong direction.

Helping mentees identify both where they are starting from and where they'd like to go positions us well for the journey. With the destination in mind, the journey can have a familiar cadence, a series of meetings and conversations with both expected and spontaneous topics focused on moving toward that destination. To get you safely to that destination in a reasonable amount of time starts with the setting of your mentee's development goals.

## Formulate Development Goals for the Mentoring Process

At the completion of your mentoring, wouldn't it be wonderful if you each felt you gained something discernable and significant— new skills, behaviors, insights, knowledge? Though new mentors often think the relationship is its heart, the work of mentoring also needs to be purposeful and directional. In fact, even if the relationship is a bit rocky and not ideal, you can still have great success (so, do not judge the success on relationship alone). Well-crafted development goals, set as the destination, always keep you and your mentee on course.

The nature of the mentee's development goal is different from a work goal and requires a fresh approach. Work goals relate to performance outputs, especially in relation to the larger department or organization. Many companies do encourage employees to have development goals, but they are usually an add-on and have less priority than performance objectives. With mentoring, development is central; it is *the* big priority. The mentee development goal needs to be translatable to new behaviors, new modes of thinking, and new skills. As a bonus, it inevitably leads to greater performance. With mentee development goals, the emphasis is also on insights arising from an "internal" focus (that is, related to personal awareness) that is essential for growth, but often not addressed at work. Mentee development goals are thoughtfully developed together through dynamic conversations. Plan on this process taking parts of one or two meetings to do this, usually during your second and third conversations. Your mentee can finalize the goal document as a follow-up to your conversations.

**POINTER**

Though new mentors often think the relationship is its heart, the work of mentoring also needs to be purposeful and directional. Well-crafted development goals, set as the destination, always keep you and your mentee on course.

In some cases, your mentee enters the relationship with a singular goal in mind (for example, "I want to be more strategic," "I'd like to lead a project team"). In other cases, there are a multitude of goals, or none at all. No matter what they enter with, your role is to help them identify a focus that is clear and realistic, making stretch steps within a longer-term direction and with a good chance for attaining success. An effective mentee development goal is one you can make happen together, given your own background and skills and the mentee's current capabilities and circumstances.

You will learn a good deal about each other as you develop the goals. Creating the goals collaboratively will deepen your relationship and produce more growth. Do not shortchange it. Let's take a look at Figure 3-1, which shows the three steps: start, shape, and sharpen, along with a mentoring example between Tomás and Bernice.

## FIGURE 3-1
### FORMULATE MENTEE DEVELOPMENT GOALS

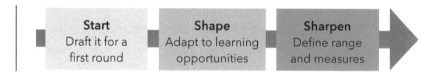

| Start | Shape | Sharpen |
|---|---|---|
| Draft it for a first round | Adapt to learning opportunities | Define range and measures |

## Start: Draft It for a First Round

Whether your mentee has come in with a starting place for their development objective or not, expect to first create a draft goal, one that will get further refined.

Begin with a discussion of the mentee's aspirations, the bigger picture of where they hope to land in the future. You can establish the setting for open discussion, unfiltered by what the boss or company might think. Create an outward look for growth, whether a role in management, a position in a related field, or deeper expertise in the profession. For a good opener, start with, "What do you wish for yourself professionally, in three years from now, and as an interim, in a year from now?"

Identify what is required—knowledge, skills, behaviors—to take on that role, with information that's accessible to either yourself or your mentee. Get a handle on this early on, to ensure you are tracking a direction that truly fits the mentee's interests. I've encountered a number of mentees who were disappointed after working toward a role, then finding out that it was not a good fit for them.

Do a gap analysis between your mentee's current skill set and experience, compared with the intended capabilities. Then determine what will require the most attention. For example, consider: To reach the desired level of competence, which of your mentee's skills will need deepening? What brand-new capabilities are required? What habits, attitudes, or mindsets will need to be overcome, requiring increased self-insight and understanding of the impact of their behaviors on others? What current, well-developed skills will prove invaluable as your mentee moves to an expanded role?

Let's consider an example in action. Bernice told her mentor Tomás that she wanted to get out of being the HR "policy enforcer" and move into a position of influence as a senior HR business partner. She identified a draft mentee development goal to become a trusted advisor to several clients, which would involve needing to help clients see the proof/benefits of taking a more long-range approach to managing performance. She would also need to learn how to formulate and raise just the right questions to help her clients think more broadly about team members' performance. Bernice felt a jolt in the pit of her stomach as she learned about these role requirements; her natural stance was to hold back from asserting her opinions to senior leaders.

Bernice's gap would require her to step up from her normal stance of using HR policy as her authority to one of using personal influence, wisdom, and engagement. She would need the skills to be a collaborator who truly understood the manager's challenges and could balance company policy with forward-looking practices. Tomás suggested her goal might still need some shaping.

## Shape: Adapt to Learning Opportunities

If you have ever had your clothing tailored, you know the value of a fit that's created specifically for your needs. Wearing tailored clothing just feels right, you are more confident, and maybe you even strut a little in the new clothes. Taking a broad, ambitious goal, then adjusting and shaping it to be the suitable size and reach, gives the goal the right bearing and sense of personal ownership.

Together, take a look at your mentee's current work circumstances. In what ways do they provide a window of opportunity to develop skills through experience? Even if your mentee is not in a "feeder" role to the one they hope to achieve, do they have a possibility to grow the required skills? For example, a website customer response analyst may not get to set strategy (that is, the ultimate target), but can gain analytical skills that build into making recommendations for clients, and then potentially create and provide a client presentation about influencing customer behavior.

Embrace the idea that as the mentor, you have no control over whether the mentee can attain useful growth options at work. Say your mentee wants to be a project leader, but is not seen that way by management. As a result, the mentee may not be offered the stepping-stone to that expertise during your mentoring process. If there is no possibility to grow from experience, based on current role or pending assignments, consider another angle for the development goal . . . one that will allow growth from experience that is within reach. For example, your mentee's manager may not provide an opportunity to be a deputy to the project leader, but is willing to have your mentee manage collaboration software and time-management tools. Your mentee won't get people-management skills, but will still get closer to achieving a goal. The point to remember is to shape a goal that includes live, hands-on experience. This is imperative, because growing skills is not a conceptual process. Without the

**POINTER**

Growing skills is not a conceptual process. Without the ability to practice through experience, the mentoring may feel too academic and be less engaging.

ability to practice through experience, the mentoring may feel too academic and be less engaging.

Discuss your own skills and background with your mentee. In what ways do your knowledge, skills, and experience provide added value to help your mentee reach their targeted goal? It is not uncommon that your mentee's current role and intended growth is not exactly what you have encountered in your career. The support you provide your mentee puts you into a learning mode as well. Yet, because you have experienced organizational life, handled setbacks, managed through transitions, led others, and learned lessons through reflection and counsel, you have a lot of know-how that will be relevant. However, if the mentee's intended area of growth is wholly foreign to you, that should be called out. If you still choose to work together, create a goal that accounts for your lack of familiarity. As an example, in my coaching work with highly trained scientists, the coaching focuses on their management and organizational skills, but not the technical ones. They still get great benefit from the coaching, but they need to complement it with access to a technical expert.

Back to Tomás and Bernice. To Bernice, shaping her draft goal based on opportunities seemed a bit challenging. Bernice worried about completing her normal duties and also assuming a more influential and collaborative role with the managers she served. Tomás helped her see how she could reshape her standard conversations with managers she already dealt with to practice new skills of gaining trust, asking high-gain questions, and diagnosing their challenges. Tomás said he was confident he could support her on this. Knowing that this was a real possibility for her growth was exhilarating for Bernice, especially recognizing Tomás's skill. This is exactly what you hope for in a mentee's development goal—real-time challenge accompanied by support. But before Bernice could get started, she needed to identify the scope and anticipated outcomes for her goal.

## Sharpen: Define Range and Measures

Target the development goal to be challenging, yet realistic, new territory, yet defined. This will keep you focused, energized, and engaged.

With too broad a scope it is frustrating to achieve it all; too small, and you will wander off into other discussions. Clarify how you will know when the development goal has been successfully achieved.

You have both taken a look at the gap and types of skills to be developed, including raising self-awareness. Now, identify what is reasonable to accomplish given the length of the program and what else is going on at work. If your mentoring relationship is open ended, select a designated time frame for this first goal, whether two, three, or five months. (Allowing open-ended timeframes for goals often leads to dwindling effort and frustration.) Break the goal into several elements to ensure you are addressing all its components. If your mentee came into mentoring hoping to make a considerable leap in role, you and your mentee might plan for gaining the specific skills that will lead to candidacy for the role as the first target. As the relationship continues, you can always add more goals. Conversely, based on the shaping conversation, new, unanticipated skills may be added to the docket.

Nothing brings the picture into clear focus like a jointly held view of what success will look like. "What success looks like" should describe what the mentee is able to do, the impact they will have on others, and the intended results to be achieved by that behavior or skill. Also consider what will be different from the impact your mentee had previously. Frame up criteria for each element; that will help evaluate the level of growth achieved. For example, if the mentee is hoping for a new role, identify which knowledge and skill set needs to be in place and how those would be successfully demonstrated as criteria for goal achievement.

At this point, the mentee documents in writing where you have arrived, and you each keep a copy. It is likely you will continue to fine-tune. In fact, some mentees further refine this document based on additional inputs from other resources, such as observing people who are proficient or speaking with someone in the know. You might also turn to reference guides that describe, in depth, what a given skill looks like when it is demonstrated proficiently (Lombardo 2009). Another accessible source for learning about skills is job-finding or recruitment websites, which lay out the details and skills needed for a specific job.

Given her in-depth discussions with Tomás, Bernice now understood that fully qualifying for a senior HR business partner role was an overreach during this six-month mentorship. Even beyond acquiring the actual skills, she realized they had to address her confidence, ability to assert herself, and comfort in advising leaders. She documented her goal with details of what skills and behaviors to address and how she and Tomás could measure success. Example 3-1 shows her development plan.

## EXAMPLE 3-1
### BERNICE'S MENTEE DEVELOPMENT GOAL

**Goal:** To become the trusted HR advisor to three business leaders within six months.

**Element 1:** Become expert at asking thoughtful, high-gain questions aimed at shifting the conversation from policy adherence to forward thinking about unit culture and performance.

*As measured by:* the frequency of dynamic two-way conversations that move beyond policy guidelines and onto broader, more sophisticated topics, to be recorded in Bernice's journal; plus, specific client feedback.

**Element 2:** Understand my internal discomfort with giving advice to business leaders.

*As measured by:* feedback from her mentor about her ability to be self-aware and adapt her behavior accordingly: plus, her own reported comfort level (on a scale of 1 to 10) after interactions with targeted clients.

**Element 3:** Assist internal clients in diagnosing performance-related issues and collaborating on a plan of action.

*As measured by:* level of client satisfaction, effective plan of action being articulated, and resolution of performance issues.

Bernice was surprised at the energy that went into the goal setting, and realized that the amount of clarity it provided put her that much closer to achieving results.

Tool 3-1 summarizes the steps used to create mentee development goals.

## TOOL 3-1
## HIGHLIGHTS OF MENTEE DEVELOPMENT GOAL SETTING

| Steps | Actions and Tips | Useful Questions to Ask Your Mentee |
|---|---|---|
| Start: Draft it for a first round | Have an open conversation of aspirations for the near-term. | What do you dream about doing in the future? Where would you like to be in three years? And, as an interim step, in one year? |
| | Identify the skills, knowledge, and behaviors required to achieve the aspiration. | How can we research the skills, knowledge, and behaviors to understand what will really be required? |
| | Compare mentee's current skill set to that required for the targeted growth. Identify where learning needs to take place, as well as personal insights raised. | How do your current skills compare to what will be required going forward? What current skills will serve you well? In what areas will you need development? |
| Shape: Adapt to learning opportunities | Align desired development targets with opportunities to actually try out new skills. If opportunities for experiences appear out of reach, find a close substitute or amend learning target. | What are the options for growth-promoting experiences at work? Different assignments? Are you able to reshape the way you do work now to give you opportunities in the targeted areas of growth? |
| | Consider the mentor's experience and skill set. As desired, shape the learning target with this in mind. | As your mentor, how can my background be a strong resource for the targeted development? How do you think I can provide new learning options that you had not considered? Are there areas where you would need others to complement what I offer? |

STEP 3

| Steps | Actions and Tips | Useful Questions to Ask Your Mentee |
|---|---|---|
| Sharpen: Define range and measures | Identify what development can be prioritized for the timeframe you will be working on this. | Balancing stretch, practicality, and timeframe, what is the scope of this development goal? What are the elements of the goal, including addressing mindset and habits of the mentee? |
| | Identify appropriate measure or feedback mechanism that will indicate the level of success with reaching the goal. | What will demonstrate you have achieved success? What are the various behavioral or outcome measures? What will be different in your performance after the goals are achieved? |

## The Mentor's (Your) Goal

Who says the learning ought to be for the mentee alone? Your relationship is in place for learning, and it goes both ways. Given your role and the seven guiding principles for successful mentoring described in step 1 and what you foresee with this particular mentee, where can you derive great learning? In managing a mentoring program, I have encountered mentors who request a mentee with big challenges, so that they, too, can be stretched as they work with those mentees. There is something to be learned through each mentoring relationship. Now, extend yourself: Purposefully come to the mentoring with a development goal of your own in mind.

Though it does not need to be as rigorous, use a modified approach to what has been described for mentee goals:

- **Start:** Draft an initial goal, identifying where you want your enhanced mentoring skills to be in the future, then use a gap analysis to determine what skills or knowledge will further your capabilities (as a mentor, a coach, or a manager).
- **Shape:** Adapt your goal given the situation and learning opportunity with this particular mentee. What is different about this mentorship that provides an opportunity to

learn something new or deepen or broaden your skills (for example, mentoring will be conducted via video across great distance; the mentee is from a different field than your own; the mentee's background is vastly different than yours)?

- **Sharpen:** Define the scope of anticipated learning and put behavioral measures against it. Identify actions you will be taking and how you can track progress with those, such as journaling, using high-gain questions, conferring with other mentors, receiving feedback, and applying new techniques.

In the creation and implementation of mentee development goals, the mentee has you as their advocate. In your case, I recommend fellow mentors as resources. In fact, in peer mentor groups, peers are mutually supportive in identifying what and how skills can be built during the mentoring process. Prioritize the skills you want to enhance (such as, coaching, asking high-gain questions, valuing differences) that will serve you best, based on what you anticipate with this mentee. Lois Zachery, mentoring guru, describes one mentor who realized that the upcoming mentoring relationship would benefit greatly from increased conflict-management skills. That mentor framed up a learning plan to increase her skill, including reading, interviews and lots of hands-on practice, and receiving feedback (Zachery 2012).

**POINTER**

Use the mentoring opportunity to extend yourself. Purposefully come to the mentoring with a development goal of your own in mind.

By creating these mentor development goals and tracking your own progress (or jointly tracking progress with fellow mentors), you will increase your engagement and motivation as well as your skill. Your mentee will experience your attentiveness. Everyone wins.

## Craft a Method for Your Meetings

Given the mentoring conversations so far, some may be thinking, "OK, when does the real work begin?" Guess what . . . you have already done considerable real work to this point. This early phase sets you up for achieving great results in a relatively short period of time. I speak with scores of mentees and mentors after the mentoring has been completed, and over and over again they describe how valuable this early work is: getting to know each other, discussing their roles, formulating agreements, and framing the goals. In fact, in a wrap-up session for all mentors in a program in which I participated, mentors were emphatic about the significance that early contracting and goal setting had. This mentor group reported considerable accomplishments were achieved due to laying this strong foundation. In short, the actions you complete while setting the direction allows you to take the mentoring further and achieve remarkable results.

Once the mentee development goals are documented and shared, or even before they are finalized, the two of you will settle into a series of meetings. Establishing the expectations for the meetings ensures an easy flow each time to dig into the work. The predictability of the structure makes it safe and reliable for an open and grounded conversation. Now is the time to confirm your earlier agreement about your meetings (how often, how long, location) and delve deeper into what and how your conversational topics will be covered.

Each of your meetings has the potential to be a gem of a conversation, taking the mentee to new places and new insights. Structure your meetings so that your time spent together is purposeful, yet flexible enough to include ad hoc discussions. Allow yourselves to delve into some areas more deeply, especially as those discussions have potential for discovery. When you feel you've gone too far afield, gently bring the conversation back on track. All the while, you are moving toward goal accomplishment (Guiding Principle #4: Be flexibly goal oriented). Avoid a meeting checklist mentality, strictly adhering to every item on a detailed list. Having a checklist mentality may cause you to brush past the dynamic that is occurring between the two of you in that moment. Tool 3-2 offers a sample standard agenda that can be used for ongoing meetings.

## POINTER

Each of your meetings has the potential to be a gem of a conversation, taking the mentee to new places and new insights. Structure your meetings so that your time spent together is purposeful, yet flexible enough to include ad hoc discussions.

In the most dynamic mentoring conversations, the focus is on new learning, mining experiences and their impact, increasing self-awareness, and forward thinking. Although these items are not typically called out on the agenda, these are what distinguish the mentoring conversation and make it so satisfying. It is up to each mentor to spontaneously identify and weave these callouts (such as, lessons learned from experience, impact achieved, increased self-awareness, next steps) into the conversation. That's the magic of mentoring.

## TOOL 3-2
### SAMPLE MEETING AGENDA

| Agenda Items | Mentor's Focus |
| --- | --- |
| General catch-up | Provide an opportunity to reconnect. Allow you and your mentee to get comfortable and ready for work. |
| Noteworthy incidences, projects, or interactions at work | Ask your mentee about noteworthy incidences, projects, or interactions at work. Patiently listen as your mentee identifies those actions that stood out the most over the last couple weeks. Discuss how they approached those situations, what was new or modified in their thinking or behaviors, and their impact. |
| Progress monitoring; pulling the goal thread through the conversation | Tie the conversation back to the mentee development goal and targeted behaviors; relate their behaviors to the outcomes that were achieved. Underscore forward progress and encourage continuing on the path toward goal accomplishment. |
| What the mentee will do going forward: field-test or practice certain skills and behaviors in real time | Identify next action steps in the learning process. Encourage their next big stretch and what they can focus on until the next meeting. |
| Check in with each other | Conduct a process check regarding your mentoring conversation, exchange feedback with one another, and discuss any needed modifications. |

As you work through your agenda, here is a memorable way to create the magic. Simply remember these three components: reflect, be in the now, and think forward. All three play a role:

- **Reflect** (to mine lessons and impact from behaviors). Have your mentee identify what stood out this past week or so: What were key interactions and the impact those had? How do those compare to similar past interactions? How did they feel going into this? What got easier or more effective? What new challenges were encountered? What made a difference?
- **Be in the now** (to introspect, practice identifying true feelings, and connect that to how it could be driving behavior, to identify what you are noticing in your own conversations). Have the mentee consider: What are their current thoughts and feelings as they describe the standout incidences of the week? What do those feelings tell them? How are they feeling about the conversation you are having? How is this conversation benefitting them? Where else would they like to take the conversation?
- **Think forward** (to motivate enhanced behaviors or interactions). Have the mentee think about: How can they handle a similar situation next time? How can they tune in internally (that is, mindset and feelings) to manage themselves most effectively? What other preparation will help them do a stellar job (for example, talk with certain people, prepare a document, research)?

As we have just highlighted, agreeing on how a typical meeting flows is essential to the success of your ongoing mentoring conversations. Yet, be aware that your meetings represent only a portion of the time your mentee spends in their overall development mentoring process.

## Establish the Expectation of Momentum Between Meetings

It is natural for mentors to assume that much of the work of mentoring occurs in the meetings you have together. However, for the mentee, the work should be continuous. In fact, your mentee should feel they are in development mode most days, punctuated by mentoring meetings as the opportunity to do deep dives of exploration. What goes on in between your meetings is where experience, interactions, and observations happen, and that's the stuff of the great conversations you are having.

Help your mentee see that they are in ongoing learning mode. You can reinforce this by discussing, in the early part of your conversations, what has occurred over the last couple weeks since you've seen each other. If your mentee does not have much to say when you first start your mentoring, persist with this at each meeting, and they will get it. They will then use the "in-between time" to do their development in action. In my book *Make Talent Your Business: How Exceptional Managers Develop People While Getting Results* (co-authored with Jeannie Coyle), a big theme is "make every day a development day." With the right mindset, your mentee can turn cranking out work into performing work with development in mind. It transforms many moments of the day into an exploration, a test of new behaviors, keen inspection of others who are masters at their work, and self-observation.

**POINTER**

What goes on in between your meetings is where experience, interactions, and observations happen, and that's the stuff of the great conversations you are having.

Bookend your conversations by identifying what kinds of experiences, interactions, and reflections will be beneficial between this meeting and the next. This way, you are establishing the fieldwork assignment, with both of you designing it. Regularly use the mentoring goal to guide the selection of those learning assignments.

This approach is very developmentally rich compared to a process where the mentor teaches or gives lessons on topics of interest and has the mentee read articles or books on the subject between meetings. This is not to say that articles, books, and other resources should be avoided; quite the contrary. It is to say that mentoring ought to be about live action, not simply topical, content driven, or academic, even if those resources are interesting. That will miss the main point for potential growth, which requires experimentation, taking risks, and increasing self-awareness.

Tool 3-3 lists potential ideas for encouraging growth between meetings; select from these or create your own to provide the best learning options for your mentee at each stage of growth during your mentoring.

## TOOL 3-3
### DEVELOPMENT OPTIONS FOR MENTEES BETWEEN MENTORING MEETINGS

Have your mentee consider which of the following actions will be of most benefit:

- Field-test new behaviors; this is first and foremost, to take actions discussed during our mentoring conversations.
- Enhance your communications at work by asking more questions, asserting your ideas, listening to others beyond the words.
- Self-observe and reflect on interactions that have not gone well (e.g., identify assumptions you were making, how you were feeling, what surprised you, what you might do differently next time).
- Make regular entries in a journal focused on behaviors you would like to modify.
- Shadow an expert to deepen a technical skill.
- Observe others in action and identify what works for them, what gets in the way.
- Invite an expert or role model to a 20-minute coffee break.
- Take on a volunteer role with learning opportunities.
- Ask for (or trade) feedback with trusted colleagues, a team leader, or a manager.

Now, back to Tomás and Bernice. Once Bernice had set her development goals, Tomás and Bernice established a regular rhythm to their twice monthly meetings. During their conversations, Bernice and Tomás explored her real-time successes and challenges with adapting the new behaviors. They discussed what it will take to influence her clients and gain recognition as their thinking partner. In between meetings, for her fieldwork, she wrote down practical yet thought-provoking questions for her client discussions. She practiced with a colleague how to turn client resistance into productive conversation. She also gauged client reactions and her own reactions to their comments. She got better and better at reading her own internal state of mind; being conscious of her mindset helped her to avoid reverting to her timid behavior.

Tomás provided perspective on what she might encounter with clients and how long it might take to see changes in their response to her. He provided feedback on her progress, which boosted her confidence. He also gave her accolades regarding her eagerness and fortitude to explore her mindset and emotions during their conversations. She felt far more willing to take on behaviors she had previously felt were too risky, as the two of them continued to identify progressive stretch actions. The momentum onward felt exhilarating. All the while, they constantly tuned into her goal statements to monitor progress. After a short couple months, she identified the extent to which clients were now using her to think through their HR concerns. Development in motion!

## The Next Step

During your last couple meetings, you and your mentee have created a clear path forward by thoughtfully creating mentoring development goals and identifying what will occur both in and between your meetings. Now you can really dig into a regular cadence of meetings where successes and challenges will be discussed, insights uncovered, and progress toward achieving goals will be tracked. Going forward, there are a number of powerful mentor approaches to be used that will strengthen your process. Though there is not a particular stepwise sequence to these, what follows next is step 4 (Leverage Experiences for Development). The core concept here is that learning is not true development until it is applied. Helping your mentee apply what they are learning through experiences is crucial to their mastery, and there are practical ways you can make this process highly valuable.

# Step 4

# Leverage Experience for Development

*"Nothing ever becomes real 'til it is experienced."*

*–John Keats*

## Overview

- Examine the possibilities.
- Experiment with new approaches.
- Enlist others for insight and feedback.
- Extract the learning.

A couple years ago, I worked with managers from a large global business to help them become more developmental. The approach was an action-learning series with one learning cycle per month over a several-month period. To complete the program each month, managers were required to participate in a short, interactive workshop with 17 colleagues; read reinforcement material after the workshop; plan and take action with employees to apply what they learned about this developmental practice; and then attend a cohort meeting with five other managers to discuss their outcomes and receive support from colleagues.

One brilliant and busy leader, whom I will call Dr. Wong, told me she had done the first two steps but did not have the time to apply the new actions with her employee, yet she intended to attend the cohort session. "Do you feel you know this new developmental practice inside and out by attending the workshop and then reading about it?" I asked. "Yes, I do. I have a definite picture in my mind about how this will work," she replied firmly. I probed further: "Would you want your employees to take charge of new tasks by reading about it, and not experiencing it firsthand?" She got my point without any additional discussion, and ended up applying the practice with one of her challenging employees to help develop him.

The following week, Dr. Wong joined her cohort group and shared her surprise about how thorny the experience was. There were unexpected emotional responses from her employee, and questions he raised that she could not answer on the spot. "What I had pictured in my mind did not compare to reality!" she told the group. Her colleagues then worked with her, asking pertinent questions about assumptions she had made and exploring potential avenues to handle it differently in the future. Others discussed their experiences as well, relating both successes and challenges. By the end of their conversation, she declared: "This was a very powerful lesson; not only about how I best learn, but for how I need to help my people grow." It's a reminder for all of us of the difference between mentally formulating our action and masterly applying the actions.

**POINTER**

Your role is to help the mentee focus on the lessons aligned to their goal, identify potential obstacles, feel encouraged, navigate the obstacles (both internal and external), and receive feedback. All of this is paired with insight-generating conversations.

For most of us, our early formal learning, which took place in primary school, was largely conceptual; studying historical facts, writing reports, and learning math equations. Decades later, as mentors, we know people learn in a multitude of ways, and that learning needs to go well beyond "just the facts." Thinking through an approach, reading about it, and planning actions gets us only so far. Having experiences in testing new behavior and interactions with people gives much more. Yet, with old habits dying hard, we can persist with a focus on conceptual learning.

A wonderful contribution you can make for your mentee is to orchestrate learning from experience. Experience is a potent teacher, most especially when it is targeted to get the lessons that are needed, and then debriefed to discern what mindsets and behaviors were used and their impact (Axelrod and Coyle 2011). Research by the Center for Creative Leadership, stretching back for decades, shows that if steered properly, experiences are the premier source of learning and development (McCauley 2006).That's one reason to avoid a style of mentoring that is just about reading books, sharing the mentors' stories, and giving "lessons." This is not the best use of everyone's time.

Help your mentee understand that jumping into experiences with narrow foresight can have limited learning outcomes. Your role is to help the mentee focus on the lessons aligned to their goal, identify potential obstacles, feel encouraged, navigate the obstacles (both internal and external), and receive feedback. All of this is paired with insight-generating conversations. A mentor's support in this discovery is a multiplier effect for much bigger gains. You will undoubtedly help leverage the learning from experience many times during your work with your mentee and increase your own skill at doing this. When supporting your mentee to get the most from experience, consider the 4 *Es* of Leverage Experience for Development, as shown in Figure 4-1.

## FIGURE 4-1
### THE Four *Es* OF LEVERAGING EXPERIENCE FOR DEVELOPMENT

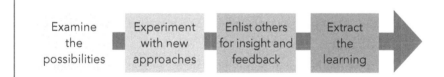

## Examine the Possibilities

At the opening of a workshop on creative problem solving, the facilitator called everyone to attention. He held a brick in his hand and asked, "What can this be used for?" The participants hesitated at first, thinking this was a trick question; then, one by one, people called out suggestions: "Build a house," "Pave a walkway," and "Create a pizza oven." "We can do better than that," he said. "Look at the brick from a new perspective, with huge potential; consider all of its attributes and how they can be used. Now, take out a piece of paper, and in the next 60 seconds, write down as many possible uses as you can think of." At the end of one minute, participants had come up with dozens of uses (such as a door stop, paperweight, engraved for a fund raiser, shelf). They did this by disrupting their typical assumptions about bricks and finding new potential for how they could be used.

Since you may not be able to count on your mentee's organization to provide an assignment that's a perfect fit for their development, take a similar approach to uncovering what experiences are potentially accessible to your mentee. Together, be creative about identifying the hidden learning opportunities in their environment; help them uncover possibilities they did not know were there. What tasks or assignments can be used to allow them to experiment with new approaches and behaviors? For example, one mentee was bent on transferring to another department because he felt his current project leader had him pigeonholed in the same boring tasks, despite his requests to be put on other duties. Then, his mentor suggested he use the very situation with his project leader to learn the skill of influencing up (something that was already on his "desired development" list). Bingo! He got reengaged at work, and week by week focused on growing his upward influence skills—something he will use for a lifetime.

You were deliberate in helping the mentee identify their goals; now be deliberate to find new assignments that will yield desired growth. I recommend three attributes that gear an experience or assignment for substantial mentee development. These attributes, described in Tool 4-1, can be your guide to shaping the experience. Identify the extent to which each of these three are present. If any one of these is lacking, consider how the experience or assignment can be adapted to integrate that attribute more fully.

# Tool 4-1
## Three As of Assignments Geared for Significant Development

- **Ambitious:** The assignment represents a reach beyond the familiar, causing a notable stretch to master new tasks, try out new modes of thinking, do usual tasks differently, or effectively manage larger or more complex demands.
- **Accountable:** The assignment is compelling and provides value to others that they count on. The implementation of the assignment is tracked, and impact is measured both by others and through self-monitoring.
- **Advocated:** The assignment is supported by others who see its worth and support the mentee in raising confidence, working through issues, providing resources, and being a sounding board when the mentee faces challenges.

Research about sourcing growth opportunities shows that for many of us, a multitude of possibilities exist in our own job environment; we just need to uncover them (McCauley 2006). You and your mentee can scan their environment to find opportunities to develop skills such as business knowledge, communications, global mindset, interpersonal relations, decision making, negotiation, and many more. Tool 4-2 presents growth-option categories. Select from these or create your own to provide the best learning options for your mentee at each stage of growth during your mentoring.

Let's consider an example of how a mentor might guide a mentee in the right direction. Cedric was an aspiring facilities manager, working for a global food and facilities company at one of its conference centers in the United Kingdom. Handling reservations and planning the usage of the building week in and week out was both challenging and rewarding, and he was recognized as highly proficient. Thank goodness for his mentor, Teresa, because Cedric's boss was so time constrained to do anything to support his growth. After a couple years in his current role, Teresa understood Cedric's interest in becoming a general manager, and they both realized there was a lot of development needed. Two capabilities Cedric wanted to advance were mastering continuous improvement processes and forecasting budgets.

## TOOL 4-2
### SAMPLE DEVELOPMENT POSSIBILITIES IN THE CURRENT WORK ENVIRONMENT

- Take the lead on elements of a team project.
- Increase scope of your work.
- Be a resource to someone who is struggling in an area you know well.
- Work in a support role for someone else's assignment.
- Increase the level of communications to your department's stakeholders.
- Manage the interface with vendors or partners.
- Resolve a long-standing customer response issue.
- Step up your leadership or innovation on a team project.
- Lean into challenges that arise in your department.
- Increase the strategic perspective of complex decisions.
- Serve on a project team from another department.
- Manage a project in your area of expertise, from identifying team members, to setting strategy, executing actions, and tracking results.

After brainstorming the possibilities within the context of his current role, Teresa and Cedric zeroed in on an idea that Cedric had been circling around for a while. He could lead a team to introduce a new, more flexible operations system, which would integrate reservations with the staffing and food components of the conference center. This would streamline the overall operation of the center and provide automatic inputs for the budgeting process. Several conference centers in the United States were using it, learning a lot about putting the system in place and its execution.

If this requested project could go through, Cedric would be developing a number of skills: continuous improvement, influence abilities, leading an interdisciplinary team, and forecasting budgets. There was no question in Teresa's mind that this had the classic makings of an incredible developmental assignment and reflected the three "A" attributes: ambitious (stretch in responsibilities, behaviors, and mindset); accountable (management would count on his success with this and provide him feedback on its implementation); and advocated (he would get support from colleagues, and from Teresa herself; she had been through similar assignments).

# Experiment With New Approaches

With the specific mentee development goal in mind, encourage your mentee to step into new mindsets and behaviors. The term "experiment" sets this up for learning, with the expectation that more refinement will be needed. Your mentee will benefit from exploring both new ways of thinking and new ways of behaving.

## Spur New Ways of Thinking

We are creatures of habit. To be efficient, many of us tend to have a "go-to" way of thinking about things, which can set us into repeated patterns. You know the adage, "If the only tool you have is a hammer, you treat everything as if it were a nail." A hammer might be right for building some things, but in a more complex world, that tool will seem negligible. How can you help your mentees increase their repertoire of thinking tools?

You start by asking questions that illuminate the mentee's current mindset, assumptions, and approaches. You might ask something like, "What are other possible ways of looking at this?" Once you've opened that door, feel free to guide your mentee through more questions designed to have them think from multiple perspectives (such as, "How do you think your client would view this?"). Be prepared with a collection of methods that might be right for the particular situation they are facing, such as those in Tool 4-3. For example, if they need to be more strategic, you might suggest they explore scenario analysis.

## TOOL 4-3
### EIGHT THINKING AND PLANNING METHODS

1. **Tree diagrams.** Analyze options and consequences of decision making.
2. **Scenario analysis.** Identify possible futures.
3. **Brainstorming.** Identify possibilities for planning or problem solving.
4. **SWOT analysis.** Examines strengths, weaknesses, opportunities, and threats of taking a particular position.
5. **Ladder of inference.** Identify underlying assumptions.
6. **Force field.** Recognize supports and obstacles to taking a specific direction.
7. **Influence maps.** Understand where power and supports lies.
8. **Design thinking.** Create innovative solutions.

The objective here is not *just* getting to an answer, even if that is a wonderful result. It is also about introducing alternate ways of thinking and encouraging the mentee to seek ways to find broader perspectives and to use thinking tools that are specific to the type of situation they face.

Remember Teresa and Cedric? To get ready for further discussions with management, Teresa suggested Cedric try his hand at a well-known planning tool with which he already had some familiarity. Not only would this help prepare him for the assignment, he might end up using the same tool again with the team, to position the project once things got started. She asked him to make a first pass for their upcoming mentoring conversation. Example 4-1 is his initial use of the SWOT analysis tool.

# EXAMPLE 4-1
## SWOT ANALYSIS COMPLETED BY CEDRIC

**Project Objective:**

Cedric as project leader for the introduction and implementation of a new operations system

| Strengths | Weaknesses |
|---|---|
| What assets and resources are in place to position this project well? | What deficits might be encountered? |
| • Cedric is already an expert at reservations systems, the largest component of the new system.<br>• He is well connected to U.S. conference centers who are eager to help.<br>• He has a proven track record in interpersonal skills and balancing demands.<br>• Many stakeholders are supportive of the plan. | • Cedric will need backup on his current role.<br>• Managers in other departments do not understand the value of the project.<br>• Cedric will need support on managing the change process. |
| **Opportunities** | **Threats** |
| What advantages does this project provide over current circumstance? | How could this be harmful, and provide unwanted exposures? |
| • It will allow multiple departments to participate in planning, increase collaboration.<br>• It will increase responsiveness to the customer, provide better cost estimates.<br>• It will keep the conference center on par with centers in other countries. | • There could be over-reliance on the response of the company providing this system.<br>• There will be upfront costs for installation; it will be a year before any benefits are realized.<br>• It could make tenured customers nervous. |

## Spur New Ways of Behaving

How you help your mentee think about which steps they will take gives them a template for action, their intention; it is intangible. How they behave is reflected in the tangible actions they take; it is quite visceral. Both are needed to develop full competence.

With the setting for testing a target skill identified, and prethinking about how to apply the skill clarified, the time is near for your mentee to dive in. Whether it is influencing senior management, leading a team, or taking a product from local to global, your mentee will need to muster the courage to take that stretch step . . . and you can certainly help with that. They can start small (especially if the actions have elements of risk, such as writing company news releases), knowing that it will take progressive steps to truly master the behavior or skill. Help your mentee visualize their actions.

Ask several questions to get the wheels turning. Two questions I consider standard are: "What actions do you intend to take?" and "What impact do you hope to have?" Using slightly different phrasing, these questions will be repeated as part of your debrief. Keep the tone of the questioning positive and hopeful rather than analytical and cautious. Providing encouragement translates into greater confidence for the mentee to be courageous. Tool 4-4 offers some helpful sample questions.

As appropriate, role play the mentee's upcoming action with them. It will take real grit for your mentee to step into situations in a new territory. Do them a favor and make the role play realistic; avoid making it too easy. Teresa did this with Cedric during a rehearsal, and she asked both tough questions and a couple that didn't even seem relevant. She was using the safety of their conversation to help him find out about the surprises that could be lurking. Cedric got

**POINTER**

How you help your mentee think about which steps they will take gives them a template for action, their intention; it is intangible. How they behave is reflected in the tangible actions they take; it is quite visceral. Both are needed to develop full competence.

anxious and fumbled the answers. Teresa handled the next part of the conversation positively, helping Cedric turn the mistakes into valuable lessons.

## TOOL 4-4
### QUESTIONS TO ASK WHEN PREPARING YOUR MENTEE TO APPLY NEW BEHAVIORS

- What is your thinking about how to approach this?
- How have you prepared for these steps? What did you learn during your preparation?
- Can you picture yourself in action with the people you'll be working with?
- Which of your established skills will serve you well as you do this?
- What particular actions will you take that are a stretch for you?
- What are you most concerned about?
- What if (fill in the blank) occurs? What resources or skills will you lean on to handle that?
- How do you want others to feel as a result of your participation?
- How will you know when you are successful?

Learning new ways of behaving through experience is never a one and done. Helping your mentee reflect on their actions is a key element of your role. You will help them fine-tune for the next time and perfect the skill.

## Enlist Others for Insight and Feedback

I once had a seasoned mentor tell me, "As a professional, I used to think that doing everything myself, never including others, showed how independent and smart I was . . . now I know, I was really hurting myself. Finding thinking partners at work is one of the best ways that I learn." It's surprising how many professionals have suffered through a level of independence that is truly limiting. Seeking out others to be a development partner as a sounding board or expert guide is one of the best ways to deepen and broaden our skills. This mentor now incorporates that wisdom into all the mentoring he does. He would say that using others as resources enables mentees to:

- Increase their knowledge of the business.
- Receive feedback from a trusted and caring source.
- Understand more about the organizational landscape.
- Receive emotional support when they feel stuck.
- Learn from others' tested approaches (and failures).
- Have someone to bounce around ideas with.

Your mentee should have a variety of thinking partners, not just you. Early in your work with them, find out how they are currently using others as resources, and likewise how they serve as a resource to others. Many mentees, early in their careers, are busy adding people to their network. Great. However, too often, their interactions with those people are simply transactional, lacking depth. Help them think about attaining true developmental partners who are working in the same environment, including trusted peers and experts as a source of information and feedback. Encourage them to create this habit for their career, and it will be as rewarding as it is developmental. Your mentee can enlist others for insight and feedback by deliberately taking the three steps as identified in Tool 4-5.

## Extract the Learning

When first learning to ski, Tasha decided to take a couple formal lessons from a ski school in Vermont. The class was small and the instructor was skilled. Based on what she was learning, each time they started down a new section of the slope, Tasha took a certain posture and observed the placement of her skis and hands. She shifted her body weight to move into the turns. She could feel herself mastering it, and after a few hours was feeling a bit like a pro. At the end of the first lesson, each student was videotaped for the next day's review.

# TOOL 4-5
## THREE STEPS FOR MENTEES TO CREATE A CADRE OF TRUE DEVELOPMENT PARTNERS

| Action Step | Mentee's Focus for This Step |
|---|---|
| 1.<br>Seek out positive and productive colleagues | • Identify talented peers who would be interested in having more in-depth dialogue and some ongoing productive exchanges with you.<br>• Start with just one or two peers; build from there. Favor spending time with them over those who are less positive and productive.<br>• Continue to upgrade your network by asking a colleague or manager for an introduction to others who do high-quality work in your discipline. Have them provide an explanation for what you are doing and request that they give good press about you.<br>• Create a network that favors quality over quantity. |
| 2.<br>Establish mutually beneficial relationships | • Be accommodating; make it easy for these colleagues or experts to meet with you.<br>• Set up talk time at their convenience, offer a favor in return, and let them know how they have been helpful to you.<br>• Build the trust factor, which comes from your reliability, transparency, and honesty. The greater the trust, the more openness there will be to discuss mistakes and challenges. |
| 3.<br>Share perspective and feedback | • With identified experts in your network, start by listening. Ask about success factors and stumbling blocks they have encountered in your field. Avoid jumping in with your problems and wanting a fix it.<br>• With peers you work with, agree to provide each other feedback. Let your peers know what skills you are developing so feedback can be focused. Because you are able to see each other in action, your firsthand observations are invaluable.<br>• Learn how to be effective at providing feedback: focus on what your peer is most interested in learning, share objective observations and the impact, and leave open space for your peer to process the feedback. |

STEP 4

The next morning, with each successive video, Tasha had a keen awareness of what to look for and could spot what the classmates did well and what needed improving. Her instructor then offered more nuanced observations. Next, her video was shown. She was surprised and a bit embarrassed by what she saw. Her body looked stiff and her turns were awkward. Funny, she hadn't realized things were a bit off-kilter. She had lacked self-awareness. Having seen this visual level of detail, Tasha was able to put feedback from her classmates into perspective. Then, her instructor chimed in, not with feedback, but with questions. The questions helped to raise awareness about her mental orientation as well as how she engaged her body. He commended her for what she accomplished as a first-timer and provided additional input. Now, she was eager to hit the slopes again, and fully master her turns.

Your mentee won't have a camera going when carrying out their new behaviors. Your job is to help them emulate "video"-level depth by exploring the insights that can come from many angles (colleagues' feedback, the mentee's close observation of others' responses, impact reported by their manager, self-insight, debrief with you), and to encourage forward thinking for next time. Learning from experience is an iterative process which, importantly, rests upon reflection after action steps (Kolb and Yeganeh 2011) . . . a step many people give short shrift or overlook. Your mentee can have a handy list of thoughtful questions and additional in-the-moment probes to use for reflection right after the experience. Then, they can discuss this with you in-depth at your next meeting. Having debrief discussions with you after testing a new behavior will become a regular part of your ongoing conversations.

Be sure you always relate these conversations back to elements of the mentee development plan so that forward progress is identified. Your role is to spur your mentee to think about things they never

## POINTER

Your role is to spur your mentee to think about things they never thought of before. Make the debrief a positive experience so that confidence for the next round is bolstered.

thought of before. Make the debrief a positive experience so that confidence for the next round is bolstered. Over time, they will be more observant and self-aware while it is happening, knowing that a rich debrief with you will follow. Tool 4-6 offers some potential questions you can ask during the debrief.

## TOOL 4-6
### QUESTIONS TO USE WITH YOUR MENTEE TO DEBRIEF A DEVELOPMENT EXPERIENCE

Select from the following:
- ❑ What was your objective for this interaction?
- ❑ What was your mindset going into this? How did that affect your actions?
- ❑ To what extent did your actions have the intended impact? How do you know?
- ❑ What were the most crucial moments for you and for others in the interaction?
- ❑ What feedback did you receive about this from others?
- ❑ Were there any surprises, either in the way you took the action or in others' responses?
- ❑ What were your successes?
- ❑ Where were the challenges you encountered in taking these actions?
- ❑ What are you most proud of?
- ❑ What additional preparation is needed before the next time you do this?
- ❑ How would you like to do this the next time?

After meeting with management, Cedric sat down with Teresa to review what occurred. "I don't think they are buying it, Teresa. At least, not yet," Cedric reported; he sounded drained. "So, you wanted an immediate 'Yes'?" she responded. He laughed, realizing his anxiety was driving impatience. "I think it is worthwhile to review this with you; whether or not the project goes forward, there is much to be learned," she said. He agreed.

Teresa proceeded with a series of questions about his frame of mind going into the meeting, how he greeted the executives upon entry to the meeting, what content he covered with them, what they asked him, his assessment of how they felt about him, what new feelings he had about himself, and whether there was someone to provide him direct feedback from the meeting. Their conversation was thoughtful and paced. It was clear the debrief allowed him to consolidate his learning.

Finally she asked, "What did you feel most proud of, Cedric?" He paused for a moment, then excitedly told her, "I am most proud of being bold enough to take the step, prepare for it, and get them thinking about something they had not considered before. All of that feels pretty darned good."

Based on your own practice, are you ready to help your mentee leverage experiences for development? Use Tool 4-7 to review how you have personally leveraged experience for your own development.

## Tool 4-7
### Mentor's Personal Record of Leveraging Experience for Own Development

Place a check mark next to items that are true for you.
- ❑ Find creative new developmental uses for regular assignments.
- ❑ Seek others' ideas for assignments that would be developmental for the skills I want to build.
- ❑ Have familiarity with a repertoire of planning and thinking tools.
- ❑ Visualize trying out new behaviors as part of preplanning.
- ❑ Seek to understand my own impact when I am testing new behaviors.
- ❑ Know the courage it takes to try new approaches that are a big stretch.
- ❑ Have a cultivated network of true developmental partners.
- ❑ Regularly ask others for feedback and provide the same to them.
- ❑ Use reflective questions to fully mine the learning from new experiences.
- ❑ Debrief my learning experience with a trusted colleague.
- ❑ Make a positive experience out of learning from mistakes.

# The Next Step

Action alone rarely leads to lasting developmental change. Lasting development also requires insight and self-examination. Next, let's explore what it takes to create the safety needed to freely examine your mentee's work life and interactions and to increase self-awareness. Because mentees find this opportunity rare in other areas of their work lives, this step becomes a pivotal component of your mentoring and an important skill for you to have. Learn the practical tips you can use to expand growth using everyday psychology and help propel the development of your mentee.

STEP **4**

# Step 5

# Expand Growth Using Everyday Psychology

*"Self-awareness gives you the capacity to learn from your mistakes as well as your successes. It enables you to keep growing."*

*–Lawrence Bossidy*

## Overview

- Know your interior processes.
- Know yourself.
- Know your mentee.
- Know how to create safety.
- Know how to help raise self-awareness.

Ripped from the headlines: Thailand, July 2018, 12 soccer-playing boys and their coach are in a dire situation, trapped two-and-a-half miles inside a flooded cave. The world watched as a treacherous and seemingly impossible rescue took place to save them; it was a race against time, as heavy rain had already raised water levels in the cave and a monsoon was approaching within days. The cave system was studied for how flooding water would completely engulf the area where the boys and their coach were located. From around the world, rescuers and experts flocked to Thailand. Outside the cave, a massive pump system was created to get standing water out, holes were plugged from above, and the opening to the cave was left open for oxygen flow and rescue divers.

Inside the cave, the boys' coach and mentor, a Buddhist who was trained in meditation, was also seemingly doing the impossible. Even after almost two weeks with no food and in darkness, he kept the boys' spirits lifted and hopeful. All the human emotion that seemed likely—panic, anger, fear, and aggression—did NOT rule; calm and resolve prevailed. Their coach understood what was needed and did not command and control the boys into lifesaving actions. Instead, he used his self-awareness, empathy, and understanding of the team dynamic to guide their actions, employing the practical approaches of psychology and neuroscience.

As a mentor, you will likely never face such a drastic situation with your mentees. Yet there is much to be learned about how to use psychology and neuroscience in practical ways to affect behavior, self-confidence, and impact on others. Even during the best of times, these principles can operate to significantly encourage mentees to stretch their limits, enhance learning, and overcome obstacles. This mentoring approach can make the experience life changing for the mentee.

The idea behind "everyday psychology" is to demystify psychological principles and make them accessible. I define "everyday psychology" as using practical knowledge of both human nature and individual people, during interactions with others, for positive effect (Axelrod 2015). Creating safety within your partnership, helping your mentee to gain deeper self-awareness, and using each conversation to move your mentee toward their ultimate goals will be greatly enhanced by your capability in this arena.

As shown in Figure 5-1, there are five important components of expanding growth using everyday psychology you should know.

## FIGURE 5-1

## FIVE COMPONENTS OF EXPANDING GROWTH USING EVERYDAY PSYCHOLOGY

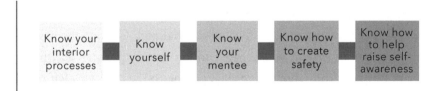

# Know Your Interior Processes

I bought my first car as a young graduate student living in Colorado. My interests were to have a solid vehicle that would be good for trekking around the mountains and had space for camping and ski equipment. Other than filling the gas tank and checking the oil, car ownership was all a mystery to me, especially what went on under the hood. At first, when something seemed awry, I would simply make a mental note ("Gee, something smells funny" or "What's making that noise?") and wait to see if something really needed fixing. After a few expensive repairs, I learned it was far better to replace the mystery with general working knowledge and be confident about what was going on. I did not need a mechanic's certification to do a great job of keeping the car running well.

Similarly, as mentors, you need to have a working knowledge of what is going on "under the hood" for yourself and your mentee—no advanced degree required.

Experienced mentors know that working only with what is exterior (your mentee's actions and behaviors) is not enough to build a trustful relationship and effect real development. Working with what is interior (your mentee's emotions, thoughts, perceptions, insights) is far more important and is key to breakthroughs in growth and development. This is a solid reflection of Guiding Principle #6: Explore the internal world as a driver for external actions. The good news is that you are already doing much of this through the use of interpersonal skills, and that provides a strong basis for expanding ability with interior processes. Let's start with a primer to increase your understanding of two aspects of interior processes: the psyche and neuroscience.

First, a quick explanation of the psyche. Each of us has an "operating system" in our minds, called our psyche. The psyche influences our thoughts, emotions, actions, and personality. Developed over our lifetime and through our interactions with others and all our experiences, that operating system is vastly layered and deeply embedded. Within the psyche lies an incalculable number of thoughts and emotions that have been filed away, including many that were not fully processed.

Much of what is in our psyches is so embedded that it is hidden not only to others, but also to ourselves. Throughout our lifetime, bringing the hidden material into consciousness helps us better understand ourselves and what drives us. It can bring order to sections of the random and disarrayed material in our minds. The more we can bring into awareness, the better.

As mentors, what is important to know is that our psyches respond to others' efforts to influence, interact with, and develop us. To varying degrees, most of us naturally defend against bringing deeply embedded material to the surface. When you are mentoring, you can adapt a style of interacting that works well with your mentee by tuning into your mentee's behavior patterns (that is, some of the visible signs of their psyche). Though you do not need to know what is in their psyche, you do need to know how to build a safe and supportive relationship, which allows them the freedom to explore "what's inside" and bring that to greater awareness. The safety also opens your mentee up to the rigors of feedback and psychologically bolsters them to embrace new work experiences, even when daunting.

Here's a small example of how this plays out in mentoring. In Marc's work with his mentee Char, he noticed that she had a habit of lowering her voice when talking about her manager. At first, Marc did not ask Char about it, and simply watched for the pattern. He sensed this was significant in her relationship with her boss. Sometime later, when he shared his observation and they explored it, she was surprised to uncover she was unconsciously trying to stay out of her manager's way to avoid any conflict.

This awareness turned out to be a pivotal insight for her ability to influence upward, something they had been working on. In this situation, Marc did not need any deep psychological training, just the ability to observe, help Char feel safe, thoughtfully bring it up, and then listen. Marc was perceptive with his timing, understanding that if he brought this up too early, it would either be innocently dismissed by Char or she would be defensive ("I don't know what you're talking about, Marc").

Now, on to a bit of neuroscience. Our awareness of what's "under the hood" also relies on neuroscience—the functioning of the brain and nervous system. You've likely seen a lot about neuroscience lately, as this age-old multidisciplinary study has advanced tremendously in recent decades. The advancements are due in part to science's ability to visualize neurons and chemical activity in our nervous system. This has particular importance to us because we can better understand the biological basis for perceptions, behaving, learning, and remembering (Kandel 2012).

Science has uncovered the various parts of the brain and how each part is related to different kinds of thoughts and emotional processes. For example, the primitive brain is related to "fight or flight," while the prefrontal cortex relates to "executive thoughts" and high trust. We also now know that chemicals secreted in the brain cause us to automatically revert to using a particular part of the brain. Two of the primary neurochemicals are cortisol and oxytocin. Cortisol is associated with our primitive brain and mistrust. Cortisol makes the person more alert and protective (very good in dangerous situations). Also important to know is that when cortisol is secreted, the chemical renders individuals less able to reason through a situation. Alternatively, oxytocin is associated with our prefrontal cortex and feelings of trust. When oxytocin is secreted, a person becomes more open to working out solutions and trying new experiences (Glaser 2014).

Just imagine if we understood how to potentially move the other person from a conversation that was driven by mistrust and "fight or flight" to one that was based upon high trust and willingness to collaborate. Guess what? Science is now telling us what is required to do this. In her book *Conversational Intelligence,* Judith Glaser describes conversational approaches that prime the brain for trust, partnership, and success. Through ongoing conversations, you can have a direct, positive impact on your mentee's neurofunctioning, shifting the processing in your mentee's brain! You can make it part of the ongoing process with your mentee when they experience high trust from you. This approach is among the tools used by executive coaches, and you can use it, too.

## POINTER

Through ongoing conversations, you can have a direct, positive impact on your mentee's neurofunctioning.

Consider the following example and what you believe is going on from a neuroscience perspective.

Peter's mentee Curt had come into the last mentoring meeting angry about how impossible it was to get cooperation from the social media group for his team that needed a survey done. Peter immediately (and repeatedly) tried to redirect the conversation and open up Curt's perspective for other options. Yet, Curt consistently responded with comebacks such as "It won't work," or "Been there, tried that." The meeting ended with little progress made about the issue.

At the next meeting, Peter tried something else. This time, he not only invited Curt to talk through his anger, he asked probing questions to further consider the circumstances that were making Curt so upset. Peter listened with attentiveness and care. Then, the tides started to shift. Curt settled down and Peter picked up the conversation—not with advice, but with exploratory questions, such as "What if there was some sort of influence that could be made on the social media group that would have them reprioritize your team's need?" The conversation went on from there.

Do you think the Peter-and-Curt example is simply a normal mentoring interaction and hardly an example of neuroscience? Think again. Consider that in the first meeting Curt was functioning from his more primitive brain, bypassing the opportunity to think constructively. Add to that, Peter, struggling to get Curt to see things differently with his assertions, was likely also having his cortisol moments. In the second meeting, Peter took a different stance and did not get caught up at blocking Curt's "fight." Instead, he brought calm and safety to the situation, and opened up the dialogue and invited Curt's more imaginative thinking. Curt was able to shift (away from fight or flight) to a more collaborative mode and identify potential solutions.

This discussion of interior processes is the first part of exploring how to expand and deepen your mentee's growth and serves as a backdrop of the balance of the step, beginning next with raising self-awareness. Before we move on, think through how, by using your intuition, self-awareness, and good sense, you have already put some

STEP 5

of this science to good use in your meetings. Use Tool 5-1 as a recap of this content with some implications for mentors, so you can do more of this.

## Tool 5-1
## Our Interior Process and Implications for the Mentor

### Interior Process: Psyche

| What's Involved | Implications for the Mentor |
|---|---|
| • A lifetime of thoughts and feelings are deeply embedded in our brains.<br>• Much of the content is outside our awareness; it may be unconscious.<br>• Content that is in our awareness serves us well in our thinking and interactions with others.<br>• More of the content can be brought into our awareness. | • Patterns you see by observing your mentee's behaviors may not be accessible to your mentee.<br>• Tread lightly when identifying a pattern. Separate out your own point of view about these behaviors. Observe more, rather than jump in quickly.<br>• Ask open-ended questions. Invite mentee to explore and make own observations; later, discuss the implications. |

### Interior Process: Neuroscience

| What's Involved | Implications for the Mentor |
|---|---|
| • Different parts of the brain activate varying functions; for example, the primitive brain is associated with "fight or flight" and the prefrontal cortex is associated with reasoning and co-learning.<br>• For optimal solutions, less cortisol and more oxytocin are needed.<br>• Chemicals are released in the brain during interactions and conversations and can guide a person to trust or distrust. | • Identify when your mentee is in fight-or-flight mode, or, alternatively, ready for broad thinking and creative partnering.<br>• Allow space for your mentee to experience and work through an upset. Provide safety, trust, and understanding of the circumstance.<br>• Use tone of voice, words, and open-ended questions to shift your mentee to more open thinking, a clearer view of the challenge, and possibilities. |

# Know Yourself

You cannot expect to support others to develop greater self-awareness without doing that for yourself. Self-awareness is your ability to consider your strengths, weaknesses, mindsets, perspectives, behaviors, and emotions and how these align with your intentions. Being self-aware has amazing benefits. Your mind becomes clearer, your actions more intentional, and you are able to control your impulses. You have a deeper understanding of your own attitudes, opinions, and capabilities and how to manage them. Self-awareness is evident in the alignment between your words and actions (you walk your talk); your ability to articulate what you are experiencing; and your physical response to interactions (facial expressions, body posture, and gestures).

When others encounter you as self-aware—and it does show up—they experience you as authentic, reliable, transparent, and trustworthy. In this way, you can be more encouraging and inspirational. Others are more willing to share openly with you, because they feel it will be safe to be open in return, that you will find them acceptable even with their flaws. This may be the biggest key to expanding and deepening growth with mentees.

Mentors who strive to be self-aware are in an ongoing learning process. They understand, for example:

- how they relate to others, and adjust their interactions for positive effect
- what they are good at, and leverage those skills effectively
- their hot buttons and triggers that put them in fight or flight, and work to move past those, ensuring more positive interactions
- that they have "growing edges," areas where improvements can be made, and they work to improve
- that regularly reflecting on interactions, how they reach decisions, and how they handle themselves during stress provides substance for increasing self-awareness.

Your level of self-awareness continues to build over a lifetime. There are always surprises, disappointments, and challenges that cause you to explore yourself further. Mentors use a variety of sources and actions as part knowing themselves better, including:

- seeking feedback from multiple sources
- pausing "in action" to reflect on what's going on
- debriefing crucial incidences with trusted colleagues
- participating in behavioral assessments, 360-degree feedback
- using coaches
- participating in leadership development.

Let's take a look at what one mentor reported as an episode of knowing himself. Hilman was a seasoned mentor and the marketing manager for a large bank. He loved the rewards of being a mentor to up-and-coming professionals in his field. This year he was asked to take on a mentee who was motivated and had great technical skills, but whose career had plateaued. He had been working with Jaqui for a couple months and was having trouble making a good connection with her. This was consistent with Jaqui's own comments to him— that although she tried to connect with others at work, peers never seemed to bond. She often felt left out.

One morning, Hilman got a text with an apology from Jaqui, saying she was stalled in traffic and would be five more minutes. While he waited for her at the café near her office, Hilman thought about the number of times she had been late—which actually had been most of them. And, he thought about the busy day he had ahead. Then, the next text came in: "Worse than I thought, 10 more minutes. . . ." Now, he

## POINTER

Being self-aware has amazing benefits. Your mind becomes clearer, your actions more intentional, and you are able to control your impulses. Self-awareness is evident in the alignment between your words and actions, your ability to articulate what you are experiencing, and your physical response to interactions.

started to brew. "Doesn't she know I am volunteering my precious time?" he thought. He decided to take a deep breath and dig a bit deeper into his feelings.

In his head, he played out a scenario where he exploded at Jaqui when she came over to the table. "Whoa, I must be going through something else," he thought. He took a minute and remembered several incidents in his past with both co-workers and family members when he felt ignored by them. He considered their behavior to be disrespectful and very painful. But after those incidences, when he learned more about what was going on, they weren't disrespecting him so much as absorbed in what they were doing. "OK, now I am getting a grip on this. I am not going to rage at Jaqui because of things in my past."

As he further prepared for this mentoring discussion, he decided he was not ready to bring up her lack of punctuality. That could wait for another time. Jaqui arrived 25 minutes late. Hilman touched on being disappointed about having less time together, she apologized, and they moved ahead with the challenges she was facing.

By the end of the meeting, she expressed her gratitude for such an in-depth and insightful conversation. Hilman would never know what could have been accomplished had he spent much of the time on her lack of punctuality and her inadvertent treatment of others. However, he was very pleased that his self-insights guided him to have a very productive meeting.

## Know Your Mentee

Seasoned mentors tell me that the more they mentor, the more they realize they need to allow the full picture of their mentee to emerge. Those early introductions are meant to present a cursory and positive impression. That's not to say those are inaccurate—just incomplete. What we usually get in the beginning is the "exterior" stuff: most mentees are not yet willing to go deep. Getting to know your mentee requires interaction, listening to their stories and reports of the week, and processing your observations. In other words, this level of getting to know your mentee takes the passage of time and conversations, particularly once your mentee is comfortable with you and the conversation flows freely. It is then that you can put the everyday psychology and neuroscience to best use.

**POINTER**

The more they feel understood by you, the more trust is built, and the more willingness to stretch and try new mindsets and behaviors.

In step 2 we discussed learning about your mentee's interests, career highlights, and ambitions as part of your early conversations. Now, you are getting to know much more, uncovering personal attributes that are not included on a resume. The purpose of learning more about them is to do your best possible job in helping them make their aspiration a reality.

As you learn more about them, realize they do not need to be good at everything, nor do you need to get hung up on attributes and approaches that are different from your own. You are not looking to develop a "Me_2.0." Specifically point your focus on underscoring the attributes that will serve them well going forward. Identify current strengths as well as growing edges. There are no judgments being made here. You will use this more in-depth picture to thoughtfully consider areas that can unlock obstacles and spur more growth. Your understanding of everyday psychology serves as a guide to that exploration. The more they feel understood by you, the more trust is built, and the more willingness to stretch and try new mindsets and behaviors. Tool 5-2 offers some general attributes it may be helpful to know about your mentee.

STEP **5**

## TOOL 5-2
### GETTING TO KNOW YOUR MENTEE MORE DEEPLY

| What You May Want to Know About Your Mentee | Questions to Identify Your Mentee's Ability |
|---|---|
| Learning style | By what methods do they learn best: reading, talking with others, experiences, reflection? How readily do they grasp an understanding in new situations? |
| Handling stress and obstacles | What is their degree of resilience when things do not go as expected? How do they manage themselves during extended times of difficulty? |
| Interactions with others | What characterizes their interactions with others: collaborative, productive, competitive? How readily do they build rapport? |
| Thinking style | To what degree do they use analytical and brainstorming skills? How idealistic or pragmatic is their approach? |
| Communication style | How would you describe their speaking and listening skills? How do they tailor their communications depending on receivers? |
| Self-confidence | To what degree do they trust their own planning and actions? How do they come across to others when presenting ideas? |
| Triggers/hot buttons | What types of situations or people set them off? How have they modified their reactions over time? How quickly can they regain composure? |
| Responsiveness | To what degree do they respond quickly, competently, and positively? When asked, what is the quality of their feedback? |

# Know How to Create Safety

How sincere and meaningful do you believe a mentoring conversation would be if the mentee is feeling cautious and distant? Not very. When you think about safety in those terms, it truly becomes a mentor's priority to ensure safety is in place.

Whether your mentee is strong and resilient or vulnerable and insecure, safety provides the foundation for a conversation to consider things they may not divulge anywhere else. Whether it is difficult feedback from a manager, a wild aspiration, a moment of pride, or an ongoing anxiety, an emotionally secure environment will allow those words to come out (Guiding Principle #2: Create a conversational safety space). Your mentee may not have the opportunity to do this in the workplace but has it with you. That's quite an honor. It is only once those words are spoken that the two of you can address what is going on. In many cases, mentors are unaware that there is not enough safety in place and that there is a missed opportunity to take conversations further, increase the relationship bond, and promote greater growth.

What will invite your mentee to fully open up? Creating safety is rarely immediate. Allow this to develop over successive conversations. Here are four conditions for creating a safe space for your mentoring conversation:

1. **Trust is in place.** Your mentee finds you credible, reliable, and honest, and has confidence that you have their intentions in mind and at heart. This is established through your responsiveness, your consistent preparation and follow-up from meetings, your candor when your opinion varies, and your raising agenda items that have no hidden elements.

2. **Mutual respect.** You each have positive feelings and admiration for each other, as well as qualities you revere in the other. You lean into your differences and put your assumptions in check. You value your individuality even if (or perhaps especially when) your thinking does not align.

**POINTER**

Safety provides the foundation for a conversation to consider things your mentee may not divulge anywhere else. In many cases, mentors are unaware that there is not enough safety in place and that there is a missed opportunity to take conversations further, increase the relationship bond, and promote greater growth.

3. **Open ears, open mind, and open heart.** You are attuned to your mentee's words and feelings and perceptive to what your mentee is experiencing. Your empathy allows you to truly understand their thoughts and feelings from their reference point. After your mentee relates a story, you respond with compassion to their feelings first, and the situation described second. Their ideas, differing from your own, are welcomed. When you do this, they feel accepted, creating even more safety in the relationship.

4. **Present in the moment.** You have no distractions. Your attention, thoughts, and feelings are focused on the mentee, their words, their nonverbals, and what they are focused on; your mind is not wandering to solutions or other content.

Here's an example of creating safety. Although Andrea was very invested in learning how her mentee Will applied new negotiating skills with internal clients, she attentively listened as he described his disappointment in the approach being taken to onboard a new team member (an unexpected new topic). She caringly responded to his frustration. When she asked what aspect of the situation was particularly disturbing, he remarked that his new colleague was not getting the attention she needed and that she seemed lost.

Andrea resisted the urge to give Will a suggestion for addressing this. Instead, she commended him on being tuned into his colleague. What came next was a bit of a surprise. Will related how often he also felt lost with no one supporting him, something that both annoyed and embarrassed him. He had not shared this with Andrea before.

The conversation took off from there. Now, Andrea would be able to help him investigate the awful feeling of not being supported and create a solution to that issue, which otherwise would have unwittingly used up his energy. Hopefully, the next time something like this is happening to him, he will feel safe enough to pick up on it much quicker. Helping Will gain awareness for the next time a similar situation pops up is an example of "Know how to help raise self-awareness."

## Know How to Help Raise Self-Awareness

When Daniel Goleman published his book *Emotional Intelligence* in 1995, there was a collective sigh of relief among organizational psychologists, like myself, around the globe. He had captured in one place what tens of thousands of pages in books and articles had been using for years to get across those same concepts. Plus, based on research, he provided proof that it really worked. He posited that being emotionally tuned into oneself and others, and using that knowledge to direct one's actions, was a dominating force to success in the workplace, from small entrepreneurial shops to massive global companies.

The core to the various components of emotional intelligence is self-awareness; it all starts there. This is a crucial skill for your mentee's future success. It is described as the ability to understand our emotions, our drives, our strengths, and our weaknesses. It enables you to sustain emotionally and socially intelligent behavior over time, despite setbacks. For your mentee, having self-awareness translates to myriad outcomes, including better decisions, greater insight into impact on others, using strengths and weaknesses intentionally, increased confidence, stronger relationships, handling oneself well under pressure, and the list goes on.

How do you help your mentee attain this? Consider the five mentor actions in Tool 5-3 that can help your mentee raise their self-awareness.

## TOOL 5-3
## FIVE ACTIONS TO HELP MENTEES INCREASE SELF-AWARENESS

| Action | What to Focus On |
|---|---|
| 1. Assess your mentee's current level of self-awareness. | • Gauge your mentee's level of emotional intelligence by listening and observing the congruency between the mentee's words, actions, and reports of what has been going on.<br>• Identify whether your mentee clearly articulates the feelings they are experiencing (Do they see their impact on others, including you; or conversely, do they blame others for not being responsive to them?).<br>• Calibrate how far and how fast you can advance to help raise awareness. |
| 2. Use productive inquiry. | • Allow for give-and-take conversations filled with thoughtful questions (see step 6 "Elevate the Power of Questions"), rather than provide a direct delivery of observations.<br>• Be patient, work through layers of awareness with small bites over time as needed (e.g., working with a very smart yet often defensive mentee, it took months of inquiry to have a break through regarding her part in the dysfunctional relationships with co-workers. When she got it, she really owned it).<br>• Pose your questions as food for thought, giving space for your mentee to come to their own conclusions. |
| 3. Have your mentee articulate strengths and weaknesses. | • Regularly probe with your mentee regarding their strengths and weaknesses in different situations (e.g., "Tell me how you think you do when it comes to …").<br>• Ask your mentee to be descriptive regarding upon what they base their assessment.<br>• Have your mentee provide examples of high standards for the skill you are discussing, and the expected impact of applying that skill. |

| Action | What to Focus On |
|---|---|
| 4. Encourage your mentee to ask for feedback. | • Guide them to tap into trusted colleagues who see them in action, to receive targeted feedback.<br>• Help your mentee think through the questions that will give them the most benefit (e.g., instead of asking, "How did I do in my presentation?" try, "In what ways did I convey my expertise with the subject? How did people react to my five key points?").<br>• Remind them that feedback is a gift, yet can elicit defensiveness. They will need to keep their emotions in check, probe for additional information, and sort out what is most important for them to learn. |
| 5. Promote a habit of self-reflection. | • Encourage your mentee to take time to regularly self-reflect, e.g., on a daily basis, similar to what the two of you do together during your meetings.<br>• Have them identify, for example, what interactions stood out from the day (positively or negatively); what actions they took during the interaction; what emotions they were feeling; what impact they had on others; and how effective they were. They can jot a few notes about this and be ready for your next conversation.<br>• Have them notice that reflections, carried out on a regular basis, cause them to instinctively modify their behavior to become more effective. |

STEP 5

Let's pick up with Hilman and Jaqui. You may recall a couple aspects that stood out from the earlier description:

- Jaqui had a regular habit of being late, with little acknowledgement about it to Hilman
- Jaqui had difficulty bonding with others at work.

For this second point, Jaqui said she tried hard by stopping by colleagues' desks to make small talk, but was rebuffed time and time again. Hilman surmised she had low self-awareness about how she came across to others and that her defenses were often in high gear, blocking her ability to see that.

Hilman asked if she would be willing to try an activity, to which she agreed. He asked her to self-observe for a week, including what she was feeling going into the interactions, to what degree she was tuned into the other person, the impact she hoped for from that interaction, and the impact she actually had.

Excited to meet with her again, Hilman asked about what she had observed. Jaqui dove into descriptions of how others were interacting with her on a particular work situation (for which she had great expertise) and asserted that they were not appreciating her. She offered no description of what she was doing, or impact she was having. "Hmmm," Hilman thought to himself, "she didn't seem to understand the assignment of self-observing . . . and her defenses were high." Hilman allowed her to continue to vent, and empathized with what it must have been like for her. He took the tact of "joining her defenses" rather than countering them. Only after his first comments of empathy for her (emotional) situation did he discuss the work issue she was encountering. Jaqui said she appreciated his support; it felt good to be understood.

During the next meeting, Hilman probed with more productive inquiries and asked her to make some "I" statements in her description of work interactions (that is, instead of always talking about "them"). That seemed to be a turning point, and he asked her the self-observation questions. She responded with actual self-observations and was able to assess the impact she was having on others. Bingo! Hilman applauded Jaqui for this breakthrough in perception and encouraged her to keep practicing this, with him and on her own. She did, both increasing her self-awareness and improving her relationships with peers.

How do you think Hilman did as a mentor? You may feel he was not direct or forceful enough, or that the process took too long. However, in this case, with Jaqui's reported history of difficulty in relationships, Hilman was able to rise above his own feelings of frustration and truly focus on what Jaqui needed, not what he immediately wanted. He established a safe environment. Trust was in place and he listened with open ears, open mind, and open heart. With an everyday psychology approach, he was able to help Jaqui raise her self-awareness. Jaqui's breakthrough was remarkable; they had both done an impressive job.

## The Next Step

In this step to expand and deepen your mentee's growth, you may have noticed that there are many questions embedded in the discussion. Questions are powerful in opening dialogue, learning your mentee's point of view, engaging them in a particular conversation, sparking exploration, and increasing their insights. In step 6 (Elevate the Power of Questions), we will consider the various types of questions, how they can be used to maximize the outcomes of a conversation, and what increases its value once the question has been asked.

STEP 5

# Step 6
# Elevate the Power of Questions

*"Positive questions bring out the best in people, inspire positive action, and create possibilities for positive futures."*

*–Diana Whitney*

## Overview

- Determine the right type of question to use.
- Layer questions for bigger outcomes.
- Be respectful when asking questions.
- Listen with interest and compassion.
- Ask yourself questions.

Bill saw the struggles his mentee Randall was having with his staff members and knew exactly what Randall should do. The problem and resolution were so clear for Bill that when he closed his eyes to think about it, he could actually visualize Randall taking those steps toward complete resolution. He even felt the sensation of Randall's hearty handshake, thanking Bill for this terrific advice. Then, as reality set in, Bill stopped himself.

Like Bill, as a mentor, the depth of your expertise is better leveraged toward creating a learning experience for your mentee rather than dispensing advice directly. This is sometimes called coaching versus teaching, or "ask versus tell," and it uses the art of asking thoughtful questions. More memorable and engaging, this approach will help the learning to become integrated into your mentee's behaviors, going beyond providing interesting ideas for them to explore.

Given a more coaching and developmental focus in today's work environment, books and workshops about the art and power of using questions have exploded over the last decade. Why all this attention to the use of questions? Questions are very powerful in establishing and maintaining a relationship. Instead of assuming you, the mentor, have all the answers, questions open up a dynamic conversation. By their nature, questions create a two-way dialogue. And, by this point in the book, you may have noticed you have been provided with sample questions to use with your mentee on each specific step of mentoring. That is no coincidence. Questions both create and change a conversation.

**POINTER**

Instead of assuming you, the mentor, have all the answers, questions open up a dynamic conversation. By their nature, questions create a two-way dialogue.

How you word your questions will determine where your mentee's attention gets focused; so, proceed thoughtfully. For example, the field of Appreciative Inquiry demonstrates that positive questions lead to more favorable and expansive outcomes (Whitney and Trosten-Bloom 2003). In your mentoring, questions are used to invite learning, gather information, and stimulate thinking. They can help you maintain momentum, demonstrate interest, and resolve misunderstandings. They are used to spur reflection and introspection, change perspectives, infuse hope, and create new solutions. This list could go on and on. Your ability to elevate the power of questions can determine your success as a mentor. But first, you need to know the right type of questions to ask.

## Determine the Right Type of Questions to Use

A while back, during a group conversation among scientific pharmaceutical leaders who were learning to deepen their mentoring skills, Sophie shared her frustration that using questions was only making the mentoring process more challenging. I asked, "Can you give us background about the situation and examples of questions you used?" Sophie went on to describe that her risk-averse mentee, who worked in another research department of their company, had a repeated pattern of approaching his clinical trials too narrowly, leading his study designs to be rejected or reworked. The nature of her questions to him were: "Have you tried using the Johns Hopkins guidelines?" "Would speaking with Kim help you see the trial differently?" Once she explained this, we could understand that she was using questions to hold back on her usual directive approach (a good thing); yet, we could also surmise that these were not the right questions to help expand his thinking about establishing the right framework for the study.

To avoid Sophie's mistake, make your questions development-worthy. The key is to consider the "quest" of your question. What do you want to achieve in this part of the conversation? What do you want your mentee to think about? In this case, Sophie wanted her mentee to reflect on the breadth and scope of the clinical study so that its outcomes could give maximum usefulness to the company, without overcomplicating or overspending. It is a tricky balancing act, and one he had not yet mastered. Her old tendency would be to simply tell him the reasons why her design suggestion would work; but she now knew he would not internalize the skill nor be able to successfully design on his own. Thought-provoking questions the group suggested she use included:

STEP 6

- "What assumptions need testing to identify the best objectives for this study?"
- "What elements need to be in place to give the department maximum return from the study?"
- "What are the most effective ways to determine optimal criteria for the study?"

There would be no quick answers, and the questions may even require him to think about it and come back to the next meeting with the answers. Not a bad thing, since he would spend the next couple weeks making a change in his thought process that could serve him well in the years ahead.

**POINTER**

Make your questions development worthy. The key is to consider the "quest" of your question.

Ask the question that fits the need in that part of the conversation. Take note that a question worded to receive a yes or no response (for example, "Did you review the checklist?") is hardly ever used in the midst of a meaty mentoring conversation. The mentee's answer would start and end with that single syllable. Instead, you want questions that lead further into a thoughtful discussion.

A useful way to think about mentoring questions is how they fit into the following four types shown in Figure 6-1. Often, from left to right, these range in complexity and thoughtfulness required of the mentee to formulate the response.

## FIGURE 6-1
### FOUR TYPES OF QUESTIONS TO USE IN MENTORING

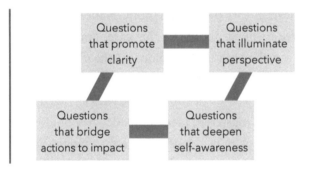

## Promote Clarity

These questions are used often at the front end of a conversation to lay out the facts or observations and ensure you both have a shared understanding. They can help establish a chronology of events or interactions, and can also spur a new realization of what occurred for the mentee. For example,

- "What is the target date for delivering the report?"
- "What is the expected revenue?"
- "Who is the intended audience for the report?"
- "Who have you spoken with so far, and who is next?"

Questions focused on clarification are important for alignment between the two of you, and form a good basis for further discussion. These also help to check your own assumptions about what might be going on.

## Illuminate Perspective

Sometimes a mentee can believe their way of seeing things is standard—the way everyone else views it, too. Help your mentee to appreciate their stance relative to others. For example,

- "Max, this step in the project is top priority for you; how does Tara view its priority?"
- "How will the department managers view your approach as contributing to this quarter's objectives?"
- "Josie, your solution is quite tailored to Jackson's needs; how will your team be able to replicate this solution for other clients?"

The goal of these questions is to help the mentee see a situation from many angles, both with the immediate issue and others that follow. In other words, you are encouraging a habit to move outside their own box, broaden their viewpoint, get into someone else's shoes, or consider how well (or not) their approach aligns with that of others.

## Deepen Self-Awareness

This line of questioning can be more sensitive for your mentee and more challenging for you to ask. They might feel vulnerable during this part of a conversation, not wanting to reveal themselves. As we have discussed, it requires trust and safety within the relationship; otherwise, they may not be fully responsive to your questions. If you are unsure, tread lightly or hold off for another time, rather than do damage (Guiding Principle #2: Create a conversational safe space). You might ask questions such as:

- "Rosa, what were your assumptions going into the negotiation?"
- "How were you thinking and feeling just prior to the interaction?'
- "Saeed, how do you believe your perspective affected your stance with the client?"
- "What impact were you hoping to have? Do you believe you had that impact? Why or why not?"

These questions help the mentee to see how their mindset or emotional state may have influenced the outcomes—for better or worse. You can take that even further by asking whether they have had a similar circumstance previously, and have them describe it. Then, there is a potential to see an ongoing pattern, a moment for increased self-insight.

## Bridge Actions to Impact

After your mentee has perspective and self-insight about the situation, they are ready to move on to what they can do to produce more effective results. These are high-gain questions that ask the mentee to do some forward thinking. It combines considering their new actions along with the desired end results. These questions have two parts: (1) What behaviors or actions are needed on the part of the mentee to (2) have results that target a larger outcome than the mentee had previously considered? Of course you can ask these questions at any time, but their responses will be more powerful once they have perspective and self-awareness. That's the beauty of building your line of questions as you go, and possibly over a set of conversations, rather than all at once. Sample bridging questions include:

- "What steps can you take to put the client at ease and then willing to move onto the retooling of their process?"
- "What will be required of you to guide the team's effort to produce a more innovative solution?"
- "What sequence of actions with your manager will help him work through his objections, and then encourage him to give you a role on that task force?"

There is no one right question that needs to be posed for each circumstance. If a question you asked seem to fall flat or took a wrong turn, no worries; try again with another. Mentors, even experienced ones, write some useful questions in advance of their upcoming meetings. Tool 6-1 provides recommendations on how you might use each type of question during your mentoring conversations.

# TOOL 6-1
## SUGGESTIONS FOR USING FOUR TYPES OF QUESTIONS DURING MENTORING CONVERSATIONS

| Type of Question | Use This Type of Question To |
|---|---|
| Promote clarity: To ensure all the pertinent facts are identified and understood. | • Ensure you understand the set of data the mentee is working from.<br>• Identify where there are gaps in knowledge about the situation.<br>• Map out the chronology of events.<br>• Identify the stakeholders of a situation.<br>• Consider untapped resources. |
| Illuminate perspective: To widen the mentee's vantage point. | • Help the mentee appreciate how others are affected by the situation.<br>• Spur your mentee to consider results that have a broader scope.<br>• Increase the mentee's understanding of how others might view their actions or contributions.<br>• Increase the mentee's strategic thinking.<br>• Encourage mentee to independently reframe their view of various situations. |
| Deepen self-awareness: To examine how the mentee's mindset or emotional state plays a role in behavior and interactions. | • Uncover the mentee's motivations, assumptions, or unconscious biases.<br>• Increase the mentee's understanding of how their interactions affect others.<br>• Help the mentee mentally prepare for upcoming interactions, especially if challenging.<br>• Help the mentee deal constructively with disappointment and adversity.<br>• Support the mentee's skill of "tuning in" to understand their own emotions. |
| Bridge actions to impact: To identify what new behaviors can lead to success on new or larger outcome. | • Encourage the mentee to identify what changes in their behavior will be required for specific outcomes.<br>• Help the mentee get "unstuck" about how certain actions are not getting the results they want.<br>• Increase the mentee's motivation to take on difficult changes through recognition of the value-add to the results.<br>• Identify that several actions, taken over time, may be needed for complex circumstances.<br>• Incorporate the mentee's greater self-awareness into planning out their actions. |

# Layer Questions for Bigger Outcomes

Have you ever thought about the number of sequences that can result from shuffling a deck of 52 cards? Unless you have Googled this, you may be shocked (like me) to learn that the number is far greater than the number of stars in the universe, or grains of sand on our planet. Considering the number of possible circumstances you will encounter as a mentor, if you want to know the right questions in the right sequence to ask, it is impossible to respond with certainty. Instead, you learn the general principles of working with the cards you are dealt, and become more expert in recognizing what approach to take in given situations.

For a productive conversation, using questions to clarify the situation and gain alignment between you and the mentee is a great way to start. Though it may seem obvious that one question follows another, a successful approach is to be intentional yet flexible. As the conversation builds, questions should be geared to the lessons the mentee has asked to learn. Layering a sequence of questions will help to expand the conversation and move it to a more valuable outcome. You may not always know where the conversation will land, but carefully pushing forward with a series of questions enriches the discussion.

As an example, I had a mentee who complained about not getting enough growth in her job. "I want to learn how to get my manager's support for further development opportunities," she told me. After a "dumping out" session with me about her manager, I could have taken the conversation in a number of directions; yet, I selected questions that fit with her stated development goal. I asked questions to illuminate perspective, for example, "How do you think your manager views your readiness to take that next step?" and questions to increase self-awareness: "How do you prepare yourself for conversations with him about

**POINTER**

Layering a sequence of questions will help to expand the conversation and move it to a more valuable outcome.

this? When you raise this subject with him, how do you think you are coming across?"

I layered a number of different questions that called out perspective and self-awareness from different angles. After two conversations of this type, she reported a breakthrough in her perception. She realized she had been whiney with him, and her boss probably felt cautious about putting her in front of larger groups. Over time, she changed her behavior and one day, seemingly out of the blue, her manager offered her the developmental assignment she had hoped for. Real progress, and very satisfying to me, as her mentor.

When your conversations with your mentee have been complex or you feel stuck about what questions to ask, try working out your questions in advance of the next meeting. Sit down at the computer or with pen in hand, review their goals, consider the four types of questions and how they are used, then brainstorm a bit. It won't take you long, but the result can totally change the conversation or even facilitate a breakthrough. Have these questions ready, but not necessarily committed to memory, because the flow of the conversation helps you to tailor what you will ask.

While many people do not put much effort into asking questions and prefer to "tell versus ask," in your pursuit of ever-increasing mentor mastery, you know the power of posing questions effectively. Tool 6-2 offers tips to consider when layering questions.

Consider Fredy, who is mentoring Jorge. Fredy sensed that Jorge had become obsessed with delivery of a strategic recommendations report for his client, to the exclusion of all his other work. Being diligent and knowing he was the department expert on these analytics, Jorge felt compelled to work all hours to get this report together in the next few weeks. Jorge had explained the importance of this work to his other clients, boss, and co-workers, but was still getting pressure to get the other work completed. What questions might Fredy brainstorm in advance of their next meeting? What would you add to the list?

# TOOL 6-2
## FOUR ACTIONS FOR LAYERING QUESTIONS FOR BIGGER OUTCOMES

| Action | Mentors Focus On |
|---|---|
| Focus on their stated needs | • Being mindful of all the possible directions a conversation can take, and concentrating on questions that raise insights and information related to their mentees' objectives<br>• Ensuring questions are productive in moving both of you toward accomplishing the goals<br>• Using questions to refocus the conversation toward goals when it goes off on a tangent |
| Add depth | • Knowing that while one thoughtful gem of a question can open up a meaningful conversation, adding probes invites a more thorough exploration<br>• Varying the focus of questions to help find the best possible avenue to resolve a concern or increase awareness<br>• Layering added questions masterfully so the mentee feels engaged and supported rather than drilled or grilled |
| Prepare ahead | • Stepping back and analyzing what will be most effective in your next conversation<br>• Preplanning and jotting down some questions for your upcoming meeting that help to create consistency from one meeting to the next<br>• Taking advantage of the ongoing nature of your conversations, saving questions for the next meeting when they cannot immediately be discussed |
| Know when you've asked enough | • Recognizing that not every part of your conversation will be in the form of you asking a question<br>• Reading the unspoken signals or asking, "Do you feel we've covered enough of this for now?" If they want more, they will tell you<br>• Judiciously providing some of your own insights, after you have sufficiently explored the subject |

STEP 6

- "Jorge, what's been your approach to handling your workload this month?" (for clarity)
- "How can you confirm that what you are putting into the report is on target for the client's interests?" (for perspective)
- "Jorge, you report being totally obsessed by this project; how has that affected your overall presence at work?" (for self-awareness)
- "What has happened for you at other times when you experienced being so consumed by a project?" (for self-awareness)
- "How can you work with your manager or others to get support on delivering against your top priorities?" (for bridging behaviors to action)

## Be Respectful When Asking

In addition to what kinds of questions to ask, how we do the asking is equally crucial. Ever feel jabbed or interrogated after someone asked you a line of questions? You may have gotten the feeling the person was not really that interested in you; more just serving their own curiosities or interests. How do you want your mentee to feel as a result of your next conversation?

Your mentee's willingness to engage fully in the questioning rests on their perception that this will lead to a positive or productive outcome. They suspend any doubt about where you are headed and trust your intentions. In short, they feel respected. You lead not just from your head, but also your heart, being considerate and pausing to take in their reactions. This is especially needed when questions get into more complex and sensitive content. Tool 6-3 offers five *Be*s to consider when thinking through this line of questions.

# TOOL 6-3
## THE FIVE *BES* OF RESPECTFULLY ASKING QUESTIONS

- **Be authentic.** Questioning is best done with a sincere interest to hear what the mentee has to say. Your genuine interest makes the conversation natural and keeps you invested, and your level of interest will be transparent to your mentee. In addition, your tone of voice, which is picked up by the mentee in the transmission, reflects your involvement, whether serious, spirited, curious, or concerned.

- **Be brief.** An effective question fits in with the flow of the conversation and stands on its own. There is no need to have a long preamble to the question followed by an explanation. That added content around the question can become the focus of their attention rather than the question itself.

- **Be patient.** Thoughtful questions are intended to yield thoughtful answers, which can take time to formulate. Often the question can engage your mentee in several ways, causing them to consider emotion, perspective, and behaviors. Exploring all of these factors will not necessarily be top of mind for them. Allowing silence and giving them time to work it through adds real value.

- **Be safety oriented.** Opening up exploration with questions can feel risky to the mentee. Safety in the relationship is one of the hallmarks of the mentoring relationship and what makes it so unique from other relationships they have at work or elsewhere (Guiding Principle #2: Create a conversational safe space). At other times, they may experience judgment, competition, or performance expectations, but not from you!

- **Be open to any answer.** Your mentee's response, whatever it is, is exactly what you are looking for. Allow it to surprise you. You may have thought you knew the answer, and now your mentee is saying something altogether different; that's a discovery bonus for both of you. If your mentee does not have an answer at that moment, that's fine, too. If it's an important question, they will think about it and come back to it another time.

# Listen With Interest and Compassion

Leading a mentoring program for over a decade, I find it both pleasing and disconcerting to have mentees and mentors tell me (with great enthusiasm) that their partner is the *perfect* match. It is wonderful to know that our mentoring program team did an appropriate pairing, they like each other, and they will want to do what it takes to dig in. On the other hand, I worry that they could fail to see how different they are from each other. Worse, they might assume they are "on the same wavelength." This could cause the mentor to take too much for granted, or the mentee to believe they are fully understood. This can lead to cracks in the relationship, a loss of trust, or diminished energy.

When you effectively use the counterpart to questions—listening—you avoid this misstep. Remember the adage, "We have two ears and one mouth so that we can listen twice as much as we speak," by the Greek philosopher Epictetus, who lived over 2,000 years ago. I would take that even further: Yes, take the time to listen, and also focus on the manner in which you respond to what you are hearing.

STEP **6**

A key to listening well is to internalize that the focus needs to be on the mentee and where their interests are. It is not a typical give-and-take conversation. You do get a lot of rewards from the conversations, but these discussions are not about advancing your interests and curiosities or getting them to where you think they ought to be (Guiding Principle #1: Start where your mentee is). As part of a discipline named Conversational Intelligence, the practice of "listen to connect" is all about allowing an open space for what is being said, without judgment or expectation. And, it invites you to explore further for full understanding (Glaser 2014). Learn to listen well, and practice on family members, friends,

## POINTER

A key to listening well is to internalize that the focus needs to be on the mentee and where their interests are. You do get a lot of rewards from the conversations, but these discussions are not about advancing your interests and curiosities or getting them to where you think they ought to be.

co-workers, and clients. It will pay big dividends in those relationships as well.

Consider the following advice for listening with interest and compassion.

## Welcome the Response

Now that you opened up the air time for your mentee with your question, how will you take in their response? Receiving what they have to say is the privileged part of this work; they may have no one else to share this with. You become the one who will help them make sense of it and use it for further growth. If they are exploring a knotty challenge at work that you identify with, you might be all ears and highly engaged—great eye contact, appropriate body language, and so on. If they are complaining about something you consider trivial, would you tend to tune out? Consider this: Joelle, a busy senior marketing manager, told me, "When my mentee started emphatically telling me the fourth version of the same story he was having with noncollaborative co-workers, I resorted to pinching myself to stay tuned in." Joelle told me she then diverted the conversation to a subject she considered more productive for the mentee (and easier to listen to). Big mistake; her mentee then came back to the story for a fifth time.

## Check Yourself

What are you thinking about and feeling as your mentee responds to the question? Lukas, an experienced mentor, takes a second or two to "go internal" and be aware of his own thoughts and reactions. Though Lukas might be formulating a solution for the mentee or having his own opinion about the mentee's manager, he puts that to the side and stays tuned into the mentee. As he listens further, Lukas can separate his internal messages from what his mentee is expressing. The result? Lukas's mentee reports that the very high level of attentiveness increases her experience of truly being heard and understood.

## Attend to All the Moving Parts

Your mentee wants to know that the complete picture of what they expressed is understood by you. In their fast-paced world, when many elements of work are disconnected, this may be the only time they can get that treatment. Mary, a seasoned mentor, asked questions to round out her understanding of Bruce's concerns about his challenges on a multidisciplinary team. She then had him physically retrace the chain of events on a whiteboard. This affirmed to Bruce that Mary had received the complexity and was in a better position to help sort things through. When a mentor fails to do this, the mentee will bring up the situation again; or worse, the mentee will move on, but take note that the mentor did not grasp the full picture.

## Recognize Their Emotion

Because mentoring conversations are often geared toward working out mentee challenges, their conversations can be emotionally charged. Put yourself in their shoes and lead with empathy, whether you agree or not. Recognize their emotion and the associated entanglements. In the end, because you have listened with curiosity, which encouraged them, and were compassionate about their discomfort, they can move on to explore further. They will be open to travel into some of the scary unknowns. That's how self-discovery happens. For example, when Joelle had the opportunity at the next mentoring meeting to discuss the co-worker situation with her mentee, she listened with compassion and encouraged him to say and explore more. He talked it through and then suddenly realized that because he felt far more experienced than his co-workers, his interactions with them had been curt and somewhat condescending, which was likely at the base of the dysfunctional relationships. This type of insight is golden. Good job, Joelle!

• • •

Listening well can make all the difference. When a mentee experiences you as fully present and taking in the multiple dimensions of what they are saying, they will trust you and take risks to explore. And, when a mentee experiences compassion, they leave the conversation feeling lighter and more confident. The conversation can be therapeutic, without being therapy.

## Ask Yourself Questions to Enrich Your Mentoring

If questions help our mentees gain clarity, illuminate perspective, deepen self-awareness, and bridge action to impact, they can do the same for us. The best mentors are in a continuous growth mode. I have worked with mentors who are managers, sales people, C-suite executives, scientists, engineers, and leadership coaches. While they love providing a benefit to their mentees, they are also in it for the learning they receive from the experience. By sharpening their mentoring skills, they go back to their day jobs with added capabilities acquired through their role as mentor.

If you had a coach mentoring you while you were mentoring someone else, what questions might they raise about your experience? How could they help increase your learning, so you could do a better job? What insight could they nudge about your effectiveness in both asking questions of your mentee and listening with compassion? What new self-awareness could they prompt? Consider Marshall Goldsmith, often referenced as among the world's top leadership coaches, author of 35 books (two of which are Amazon's top selling leadership books of all time). Goldsmith has hired someone to call him each day to ask him growth-provoking questions (Morgan 2016). If it's good enough for Goldsmith, a premier coach, it can work for us, too!

Some mentors are fortunate to have peer mentors who work with them in this way, and I highly recommend this arrangement. However, it is also a very useful approach to have questions for yourself that you have developed. It may seem a little odd at first, as it is more straightforward to simply reflect on what transpired with your mentee and take notes; however, as I described earlier, questions create an engaging dynamic.

Tool 6-4 provides a starter list of questions to ask yourself. Add your own questions that are relevant to your current mentorship.

## TOOL 6-4
### SAMPLE QUESTIONS TO ASK YOURSELF TO ENRICH YOUR MENTORING

- Is my view of my mentee's goals consistent over time, or is it changing?
- What is my understanding of the significant aspects of my mentee's work life?
- What is the comfort level in our conversations—mine and my mentee's?
- If my questions are not having the desired impact, what might be contributing to the situation?
- What is the evidence that my mentee trusts me and is willing to take risks in our conversations?
- What is evidence that I am using the four types of questions appropriately (or not)?
- How does my level of trust in my mentee impact my effectiveness with questioning and listening?
- How have I moved past my own biases about my mentee's challenges, and focused on developing a solution that could be theirs alone?
- What is the evidence that I am listening to my mentee with compassion (or not)?
- What am I learning about myself in this process of questioning and listening?
- Other questions you have developed:

## The Next Step

In these last few steps, we have identified ongoing actions (leveraging experiences, expanding growth, and elevating the power of questions) that are used throughout the mentoring process to truly distinguish you as a masterful mentor. Likewise, the next step continues to add depth and breadth to your skill. Extend and cement the development by guiding your mentee to experience a variety of learning approaches. Dig into step 7 (Diversify the Development Methods) to understand the additional learning approaches that will augment your mentee's growth and make the mentoring process even more engaging and memorable.

# Diversify the Development Methods

*"Sour, sweet, bitter, pungent, all must be tasted."*

*–Chinese proverb*

## Overview

- Recognize what is effective for development.
- Explore options for development.
- Diversify your own development as a mentor.

Are you familiar with the success of cook-at-home meal delivery services? This is an industry that has rocketed over the last decade in North America, Europe, Asia, Australia, and elsewhere. For busy singles, couples, and families, it gives them ready access to a variety of meals they create themselves. And despite the cost of these ongoing subscriptions, which many people object to, the industry has attracted a devoted segment of the population who cross that cost barrier, enticed by the variety, new taste exposure, ease of use, and the hands-on nature of the meal preparation. They have an appetite to learn different cooking methods and have new taste experiences that make going home to the evening meal inviting. No question, the variety increases its appeal (Melton 2017).

You can use a similar approach to mentoring to keep your mentee enticed in the learning process, making them hungry to try different types of development—a variety of experiences that engages and grows them. While this approach relies on you to offer various development options, this chapter provides you with a bounty of great ingredients, and you can add your own to the mix. Diversifying development approaches begins with understanding what characterizes a highly valuable development option. Then you and your mentee are ready to explore an array of options, uncovering which of these will be most appropriate and satisfying for your mentee.

## Recognize What Is Effective for Development

You've already got a satiating development process going on with your mentee: rich and focused conversations, field-testing new behaviors, taking on stretch assignments, talking with peers or experts, and increasing self-awareness. All of these constitute the heart of your mentoring. Many mentors would stop there; however, you can take this further. Because your mentee is in a dedicated learning experience with you, adding more value by bolstering that with additional learning methods will make the growth even more significant and exciting. Yet given the sizable number of development options and tools (including webinars, assessments, podcasts, projects, online trackers, and volunteer work), it is tough to know what will work best. How will you select options that give your mentee something that is tailored for this situation and yields the highest return for the investment of time? Will you know it when you see it?

When it comes to supplementing your mentoring efforts, consider development approaches that fit the four standards shown in Figure 7-1.

### FIGURE 7-1
### FOUR STANDARDS FOR SELECTING A DEVELOPMENT OPTION

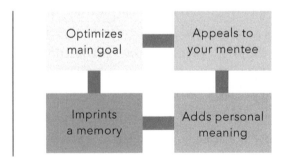

## Optimizes the Main Goal You Are Working On

Look for development that deepens what you are already have in progress, rather than take the mentee in another direction. For example, avoid adding too much focus on development based on hot new articles that are not related to the mentee's purpose, even when they are fascinating to you. Your time together is too precious for many of these topical conversations. This is a reminder of Guiding Principle #1: Start where your mentee is. Stay focused on the main goal, giving them greater context, helping them understand how others are affected by their actions, or providing lessons learned from experts. In short, this standard focuses on providing additional insight that ensures the mentoring goal is met with even greater depth and breadth. As an example, one mentor whose mentee was working on a team project that was going to create department-wide changes in procedure explored these options with his mentee:

- Learn how to use tools such as process mapping to help plan out the sequence of changes.
- Construct an impact scenario to share with the entire team and have them build scenarios as well.
- Conduct stakeholder interviews to learn about their needs during the change.

## Appeals to Your Mentee

Serving a luscious steak dinner at your home won't get a vegan guest excited. Likewise, look for development options that are naturally appealing to your mentee. While people learn best through a mix of methods, our learning preferences vary. What is enjoyable for some is a labor for others. Does your mentee learn most readily from experimenting, reading and reflecting, listening, or watching others? And, though decades of studies have tried to pinpoint how to develop people based on their personal learning styles, several meta-data studies on learning styles upended that approach, concluding that trying to fit a learning option to a person's learning style has negligible impact. (Goldhill 2016). The best way to discern what is appealing is to simply ask, which also adds to their buy-in of taking on the development. Given a group of mentees who are all developing skills to get the most valuable responses from customer focus groups, their astute mentors differentially suggest options that fit their mentee, such as watch a video, interview an expert, listen to a podcast, increase perspective by participating in focus groups themselves. Consequently, do not be disappointed if your mentee did not want to read a favorite article; simply look for options that appeal to a different style of learning.

## Adds Personal Meaning

Look for options that are personally meaningful for your mentee. Well-known author, speaker, and talent development expert Josh Bersin tells us that when we take on work that calls to us and feels purposeful, we do better work. Research shows that people who find their work meaningful have higher performance, stronger relationships, and are more engaged (Bersin 2015). Those are phenomenal outcomes to having work that is purposeful. And, given that only a minority of people (28 percent, as highlighted in this Bersin article) find their workdays meaningful, this approach can be wonderfully enriching for your mentee.

Consider that although your mentee's primary mentoring goal may outwardly seem somewhat disconnected to their personal passion, you can help them uncover what development action creates a connection to greater meaning. This supports Guiding Principle #4: Be flexibly goal oriented. For example, if the mentee is working on team leadership skills and also has an abiding interest in the environment, have them step up on that task force at work that is focused on increasing the company's environmentally friendly practices. Or, if your mentee is a passionate fitness buff, find a way to tie that together with their goal of learning how to influence (for example, head a workforce campaign to encourage employees to adopt more healthy habits). Tying personal purpose to the development option is an incredibly powerful combination that has your mentee take the learning even further.

## Imprints a Memory

Look for development options that will create long-lasting impact. Remember high school science lab? The chemistry teacher took concepts off the page and blew them up in the lab.

My chemistry class really left quite an impression on me, and that teacher is one for whom I can actually still remember his first and last name. Given that your mentee has so much coming at them each day, ensure the options selected truly make the lesson sticky. Several qualities of the development experience that make it sticky include:

**POINTER**

Although your mentee's primary mentoring goal may outwardly seem somewhat disconnected to their personal passion, you can help them uncover what development action creates a connection to greater meaning.

- uniqueness—an experience the mentee has never tried before (and many others haven't either), such as visiting an innovative robotics facility to learn strategic perspective
- emotional elements—this option could have hidden surprises or pulls at your heartstrings, such as interviewing someone (not just watching one) who thrived after a natural disaster, as a way to learn about resilience
- credibility—exposure to a professional who is best-in-class, such as taking an online class in writing from James Patterson (yes, when this book went to press, MasterClass offered that option; MasterClass 2018).

STEP 7

# Explore Options for Development

"It's just OK," Denise responded with hesitation during a check-in with me about how her mentoring relationship was going. Denise was mentoring Celia, a talented, creative web developer whose aim is to head her department in two years. However, her attempt to use the same approach with Celia that she had with her last two mentees was not working. Denise was close to writing Celia off as maybe not really being motivated with mentoring. "Last year, when I recommended a particular book to Joe, it really sparked him and led to intense conversations and lots of application on his part. This year, knowing Celia's interests, I recommended a great book to fit her needs; she reviewed the inside cover on Amazon and said maybe she'd read it in the future. I tried again with trending articles on innovation and, again, it went nowhere." Denise eventually did catch on: Although she consumes books in volume, her mentee Celia was not much of a reader and preferred other avenues of learning. Denise had to separate out her learning style from Celia's.

The options for development that complement your mentoring can be numerous. The following 11 options are described, giving information about learning situations with which they resonate and the general steps for implementing them. As you and your mentee explore, you may want to test them against the standards for selecting development options provided here, so that the option you select meets at least two, if not all four, of the standards.

## Journaling

This is used to increase self-observation skills and reflection and to track progress. Mentees who enjoy reading and writing find this particularly appealing, though as a development option, it can be used universally by all mentees (and mentors). The approach uses a bit of structure, which your mentee creates; sample ground rules include:

- Make entries at the beginning or end of each day.
- Focus on incidences related to the primary mentoring goal.
- Provide description of what occurred, how you felt, and the impact that was made.
- Allow time to review and reflect.

A recurring question for journal reflection is "What am I learning about myself? How do I see myself differently?" As the mentor, there is no need to ask what your mentee is writing about.

Instead, use more questions in your conversations that address their "internal processes," such as their mindset going into situations, feelings, obstacles they are encountering, willingness to take risks, and newfound confidence. These questions will both draw out what they have already written and encourage them to do further journaling.

## Coach Others

This is used for mentees who want to solidify their knowledge or expertise by helping others to learn without direct teaching or telling (that is, facilitate the other person to make their own sense of it and apply the knowledge). This is useful for mentees in a team leadership, management, or training role. Prior to the coaching of others, discuss coaching methods with your mentee, using a coaching modality as you do this. For example, instead of telling your mentee what to do, ask what they believe will be most effective. Ask about the actions they will take as well as about their feelings while doing this. If they need more help, brainstorm ideas together. Test out various scenarios they may encounter, including handling defensiveness and objections. Help them understand the power of leveraging questions, how to observe and respond to nonverbal cues, and how to use paraphrasing. At your next meeting, debrief the coaching session they conducted, identify what new awareness they have about what was required of them, and generate ideas for how they can continue to improve.

## Reverse Mentoring

As a specific type of coaching, reverse mentoring is when your mentee provides development for you, a peer, or someone else. The learning targets can be enhancing interpersonal relationship skills or facilitating learning in others without direct teaching or telling. It is a reciprocal arrangement where your mentee provides the other person an opportunity to learn more about a discipline in which they are particularly skilled. The typical focus is on social media, technology, or current trends in their field. Do not be confused by the use of the term *mentoring* here. There is not an expectation during this reverse mentoring that your mentee is establishing an all-out mentoring process, as you are. Instead, they are focused on specific subject matter, using the principles of coaching for a relatively short term. Participate only if you have a sincere interest in this, or it could be detrimental to your ongoing mentoring. If this is not of interest to you, no worries; they can set up this reciprocal arrangement with someone else. It can be a very satisfying and growth-promoting experience for your mentee.

## Interview Experts

This is used to deepen technical knowledge and perspective. Guide your mentee to think through their skills in this area and pinpoint where they'd like to improve, plus what else they would like to learn. Have them prepare a set of questions that uncovers areas where they'd like to learn more while also making good use of the expert's time (avoid spending time with the expert on the basics). They should also prepare introductory remarks so that proper expectations are set with the expert and the expert knows how to tailor remarks. A well-known financial and consulting institution has their mentors and mentees use this process regularly to help mentees understand the workings of this complex organization. After the meeting with the expert, have them debrief their learnings with you and post in their journal. If they have not already done so, they should send a thank-you note to the expert; this is a good way to build an ongoing relationship.

## Site Visit

Use this to attain a new vantage point on how their own business functions, given a different context. Professionals learn about how the other company operates and gets results. You may be aware that among the best known site visits, where much learning has been transferred, are the electronic and manufacturing facilities in

Japan. Factory visits are so popular in Japan that TripAdvisor actually provides a long list of such tour options. For your mentee, you probably won't find a preset visit plan. This development option requires setting up the visit, and you can help find the site through your connections (either directly or through others). Your mentee should identify objectives for the visit. During the visit, they should focus flexibly on those objectives as well as other elements the host wants to offer. To maximize the value of the site host, they may want to include others from their department on the visit. This adds to their presence within their company, and managers will take note. As with other methods, be sure to debrief, ask about new perspectives gained, and discuss how they can apply what they've learned.

**POINTER**

Site visits can enable your mentee to attain a new vantage point on how their own business functions, given a different context. This development option requires setting up the visit, and you can help find the site through your connections (either directly or through others).

## Create Visuals

This method is very useful for helping the mentee see the bigger picture of context surrounding the situation and requires no artistic talent. Some visual methods can be done on the back of an envelope; some require hours of thinking and researching. You and your mentee then review the visual together. As an example, creating a simple time line and answering the question, "What happened and when?" allows the mentee to map out a challenge in detail and then discuss it with their mentor, who might ask questions such as "What assumptions did you make going into that meeting?" "Where did the planned actions start to go off track?" "What possible invisible influences are not depicted here?" A favorite visual of mine is Stakeholder Mapping, which can be used to identify the sources of influence and what they are looking for within a particular project. Any of the visual methods will open up a conversation, provide new vantage points, and supply your mentee with yet another tool they can add to their kit.

STEP 7

## Role Play or Rehearsal

This method is used to help your mentee get ready for challenging interactions with others (for example, a negotiation or influencing) or for presentation (such as, sales report to management). It creates a link from "thinking" about what can occur to actually "feeling" it, viscerally. In the live interaction with you, they can hear their own words, experience their emotion, and be subject to your responses and questions to practice the live interactions. It builds the experience as well as self-knowledge. If there is an opportunity, video the session for your mentee, which serves as its own source of feedback that can be reviewed again and again. As an example, for 911 operators, mentors work with their mentees regarding the myriad calls they could receive, ranging from life-threatening situations to a cat stuck in a tree. Rehearsal and role play can be a primary tool for learning their profession. Tool 7-1 provides a format for a role play. Wrap up the sessions by highlighting your mentee's plans for doing this in real time.

## Experts on Video

We do not need to learn from experts solely through books and articles. Any number of services provide experts on video, so we can hear these ideas straight from the source. For example, billed as "ideas worth spreading," TED Talks provide in-depth focus on singular topics by subject matter experts. Video recordings from various other sources (including subscription services targeting wide-ranging topics of interest for those in the work world) are usually curated to make access by topic more manageable. These can be used with your mentee both for the content and as a role model on speaking and presentations. Your role is straightforward with this one. Help your mentee zero in on what topics and speakers will be most beneficial, given their goal. Watch the same video yourself. At your next conversation, debrief the value of the video content and how it can be transformed into actions or self-insights for your mentee.

# Tool 7-1

## Format to Conduct Role Plays

| Action | What to Do |
| --- | --- |
| Identify the situation | • The mentee describes what they anticipate in the "real" situation they are facing (for which they are practicing): the setting, who will be present, personalities and points of view, what new behaviors they will be testing out, and other relevant information. |
| Gain clarity | • The mentor asks questions to get additional context and details.<br>• Identify what impact the mentee hopes to have and what will be achieved in the interaction. |
| Prepare for your roles | • Learn more about the stance the mentor should take and the likely hot buttons of the role being played.<br>• Each take some time to think through the points they want to convey, identify questions they will raise, and consider how they might handle challenges encountered. |
| Conduct role play | • Establish the length of the role play and who will start the interaction.<br>• Proceed with a give-and-take interaction that mimics the anticipated real situation.<br>• Allow for intensity in the interactions and asking tough questions; use gestures and facial expressions to make it real. |
| Debrief what occurred | • Mentor asks the mentee what stood out about the interaction.<br>• Explore how the mentee felt they conducted themselves in the interaction—what was done well and what could be handled more effectively next time.<br>• Mentor invites mentee to ask questions and provides feedback.<br>• Mentor brings all the pieces together—mentee's content, interaction style, professional demeanor, and how the mentee handled surprises or challenges. |
| Plan for another round to apply learning | • Based on what the mentee learned from this role play, plan on additional role play(s) with mentor or others, or simply rehearse out loud.<br>• An option for another round is to have mentee and mentor switch roles and have mentee provide feedback to the mentor. |

## Pair Up With a Colleague

This is used to learn from a co-worker, increase interpersonal skills, share accountabilities, and increase capability in co-creation. Depending on the formality in their workplace, your mentee may need to pass this by their manager. This starts with identifying the specific purpose of what is to be gained by this partnership on part of a job, special assignment, or targeted task. Then, an agreement is formulated regarding how your mentee and their work partner will work together, share responsibilities, handle differences, manage time and performance, and check progress for the targeted length of time.

Your mentee should carefully identify their partner, choosing someone from whom they can learn and who has good work habits. Your mentee should expect to share knowledge and feedback, co-create solutions, and be enthusiastic about the process. This pairing can vary in length; a half day, several times during a week or two, or longer. Your debrief can focus on how they are managing expectations, what they are learning about the discipline, and how they see themselves differently.

## Volunteer Work

This can be used to gain exposure to a wide range of potential experiences that may not be available to your mentee on the job. Everything from customer relations, negotiations, leadership roles, marketing, budget administration, policy development, and more can be found in volunteer roles.

**POINTER**

Volunteering can be used to gain exposure to a wide range of potential experiences that may not be available to your mentee on the job.

I previously worked with an executive who took a volunteer role as chairman of a board of a public organization, and used that experience to help demonstrate his CEO capabilities for his next professional move in a corporate setting. This is a significant commitment. Your mentee should select a volunteer organization carefully and commit only to a well-run organization, and one that understands their developmental interests and can deliver on them. Regularly check in on how the volunteer work is going, what is being learned, what obstacles they are encountering, and how they can transfer that learning to other parts of their work life.

## Change Perspective

This is used to think more broadly, understand biases, solve problems, and collaborate better with others. When you find your mentee is stuck on an embedded problem that could benefit from different vantage points, use a process called "reframing." Have them identify the challenge from their own perspective and write it down (such as a customer being inflexible about pricing). Then, have them jot down the same issue from several other perspectives. For example, they could write the issue from the perspectives of their department head, customer, the accounts manager, and customer response team. Now, have them write a viable solution from each of the other perspectives. Then, given the multiple perspectives, have them create a new solution they could apply. You can use this with your mentee during one of your meetings and ask them to use it again when a new situation arises.

We have reviewed only 11 of the scores of methods that diversify your approach to development. Build a reference file for yourself and add other methods you have used or learned about from other mentors. Ask other mentors what was particularly helpful for them to advance growth with their mentees and themselves.

Tool 7-2 summarizes how to approach the general standards for identifying a significant development option and selecting the one that suits your mentee and will inspire further learning.

# Tool 7-2
## Diversifying Your Mentee's Development Options

Apply criteria to identify a development option that works for your mentee:
- Pinpoint where more learning would allow your mentee to add depth and breadth in achieving their mentoring goal.
- Seek out learning methods that are most appealing to them, or that they would be willing to try.
- Uncover: If their life were filled with purpose, what would they be doing? What kinds of actions or principles really bring meaning to their life and work? Then, explore how development options could be connected to this.
- Consider what would make this development most memorable.

Determine one or more complementary development options aligned with the development goal:
- Review options provided in this chapter or co-create other development options and begin to craft the development action.
- Determine scope (how much time to be spent, over what period of time) of this development action, given the value to be realized.
- Help ensure success: Pinpoint the objective, help your mentee set expectations for what can be accomplished, identify any prework needed to make the most of the experience.

Always debrief the development experience so that the learning sticks and makes the entire experience far more likely to result in lasting behavior change. Ask questions focused on:
- Where are they growing?
- What are they learning about themselves?
- What will be the impact of this learning on their performance?
- How can they further apply these newly expanded skills?
- How does it bring your mentee closer to achieving their mentoring goal?

Let's return to Denise and Celia. When Celia was not interested in reading a book or article, Denise wondered how committed Celia really was to the mentoring process. Now that we have explored the criteria for choosing complementary development as well as a list of such options, what approach would you recommend Denise take? Given that the options mentioned in this chapter comprise only a partial list, your answer may introduce additional development ideas. Personally, there are a couple options that come to mind:

- Denise might explore with Celia that she have a conversation with an expert outside her company, such as the head of a web design unit at an ad agency (which also acts as a mini site visit). This would open her perspective as to what is required when juggling multiple clients and a team of creatives. Denise could then help Celia identify competencies needed to add to her long-term plan.

- Denise could support Celia's effort to provide ongoing coaching for a department member who wants to grow, really fine-tuning her coaching skills (such as listening and asking productive questions), so Celia is further prepared for an important element of managing others. Denise could guide Celia to ask that person for feedback regarding how the coaching is going and what else would be helpful to the team member.

With Celia's experimentation in a plan like this, imagine how the mentoring would take on a broader range and expand the ongoing conversations they have. Celia will find additional ways to grow and test new behaviors, and Denise will experience Celia as fully committed.

## Diversify Your Own Development as a Mentor

What about you and your development? Are there actions you can take to diversify your growth as a mentor? Of course there are. In fact, as part of post-mentoring program assessments I have led (completed by mentees and mentors after they have concluded a mentoring program), some of the most gratifying comments come

**POINTER**

Mentors who
continuously
grow are great
role models for
mentees and other
professionals.

from the mentors regarding how much they are learning—both new skills and about themselves. And the proof is in their continued enthusiasm to voluntarily rejoin the mentoring program year after year. Mentors who continuously grow are great role models for mentees and other professionals. When their nonmentor colleagues commend them and say, "I wish I could mentor, I just do not have the time," these mentors just smile, knowing how much value the work gives them, that they gladly participate and are better for it.

As with your mentee, there is a wide menu of options for your own development. Here is an array of development options specifically geared to mentors.

## Create Your Mentor's Toolkit

Set up an e-folder or a section in your library for resources. Given that you may mentor again and again, new interests and challenges may crop up with each new mentee. Create a habit of storing those materials recommended by others. Be on the lookout for tools, videos, and models that may be of value for use with your current and future mentees. If you are part of a mentoring program, you may already be provided with a tool kit, but don't stop there. Search for content focused on, for example, growing leaders, technical expertise, emotional intelligence, decision making models, project management, innovation, strategic thinking, and navigating politics.

## Participate in a Mentors' Peer Group

Following an approach used by executive coaches, a number of mentoring communities have mentors' peer groups. The purpose is to coach one another given current mentoring situations, raise insight, and share knowledge. With confidentiality assured, each mentor has an opportunity to present a case, while other mentors use coaching approaches to help the presenter explore issues, their internal mindset, and potential approaches. The peers use insight-raising questions rather than provide direct solutions (that is, this is not intended to be a problem-solving forum). The focus is clearly on each mentor's growth, rather than on the mentee. Groups are kept small (five to seven members), ground rules are set, and they meet at a regularly scheduled time, often virtually. Often, an experienced coach or facilitator guides the group. Tool 7-3 can help create an approach that works for you and your peers.

## TOOL 7-3
### SAMPLE FORMAT FOR MENTORS' PEER GROUP

- Form a group of 5-7 peer mentors and identify a group facilitator.
- Plan regular meetings (e.g., monthly); approximately 1 hour.
- Use a conference line or video chat to ensure most mentors will attend each meeting.
- Preplan the meeting, identifying one or two mentors who will prepare to present their case.
- Sample meeting agenda:
  ° Each mentor provides a very brief update on the progress of their mentoring.
  ° One or two mentors present their case:
    - Describe specific interaction with mentee and approach you applied (e.g., using high-gain questions to help increase mentee's self-awareness).
    - Provide anticipated outcome you hoped to achieve with the mentee.
    - Explain what happened and the impact for the mentee and yourself.
    - Identify challenges (e.g., complications, hurdles, surprises you encountered in addressing the mentee) and/or successes (e.g., a breakthrough with the mentee).
  ° All other mentors use a mentor's approach to respond to the case presenter (e.g., use thought-provoking questions, help to open up perspective, brainstorm ideas for additional approaches); identify what you learn from the presenter's approach.
  ° Meeting wrap-up: each mentor peer describes key learning from that day's conversation and what they anticipate for the next steps in work with their mentee.

STEP 7

## Take Assessments

Find a professional source to take one or more assessments to learn more about yourself, what styles of operating and thinking distinguish you, and how you differ from those with other styles. Generally, such assessments are administered by someone certified in that particular assessment tool, with that expert providing you the results and feedback. It is a bit of an investment, and yields benefits not only related to being a great mentor, but also to your job and other relationships.

One of most used assessments in the workplace worldwide is the MBTI (Myers–Briggs Type Indicator). Whether you use this one or not, know the value of assessments that have validity and reliability tests conducted regularly to ensure its quality. Results help you understand your mode of operation compared to others, and raise awareness of your tendencies, strengths, and blind spots, and importantly, how you can bridge to others. Another assessment is the DiSC Profile, which helps its users better understand their preferences, adapt to others, and improve their communications with others. These two are just a small sampling; there are a couple dozen other highly reputable and well-validated assessments. Choose one that interests you and that you feel is best positioned to help you as a mentor and a coach.

## Tap Into Professional Coaching Methods

As a discipline, executive leadership coaching provides a countless number of resources, studies, tools, books, and videos. While the certification process for executive coaching is extensive and takes years, the methods used by executive coaches are often aligned with what mentors do. Skills such as listening, providing empathy, building trust, and holding confidences are shared by the best mentors and coaches alike. Peruse the International Coaches Federation website (www.coachfederation.org) to gain access to research and articles on methods used. Take a look at journals for executive coaches as well.

## Take Training on Cultural Awareness and Valuing Differences

Every year, the world is more and more interconnected. Cultures, countries, and ethnicities all meet and mingle. How well do we appreciate, respect, and value our differences from others? Years ago, on a business trip to Japan, during the first day of meetings I was asked if I'd like a boxed lunch, and responded affirmatively. Similar to meals at many corporate meetings, I expected something like a small salad, a sandwich, and fruit, all packaged in a disposable box. Instead, I was astonished to receive an exquisitely decorated lacquered Bente box, filled with rice balls, several types of fish, sushi, marinated vegetables . . . in all, 16 colorful and distinctive items. Thinking I had been given someone else's lunch, I told my host that I had asked for a "regular" boxed lunch. Clearly, my expectation for a boxed lunch was way off. If I'd had an open mindset, I would not have been so surprised.

When you have a mentee whose world is so different from your own, you need to be tuned in and open. Consider it part of your job description (Guiding Principle #1: Start where your mentee is), not the other way around. Participating in training on cultural awareness or valuing differences opens up your thinking, has you check your assumptions, and makes you aware of what is called "unconscious bias." You become more available to your mentees and more appreciative of them. These training programs may be offered by your company or found online.

You want to be the most masterful mentor possible (Guiding Principle #7: Bring your best self). The more you develop, the more skills and resources you have, the more you can offer your mentees. Your personal growth not only makes you more capable, but it also it makes you more inspiring—part of the mentor magic.

STEP 7

## The Next Step

The last few chapters have been dedicated to mentoring methods and approaches you are using throughout the mentoring process that lead to remarkable results (leveraging experience for development, expanding growth by using everyday psychology, elevating the power of questions, and diversifying development methods). Throughout the entire process, you are continuously enlightened by the use of the seven guiding principles. Next, let's consider pushing even further by having your mentee enhance crucial influence skills. Increased ability to influence will allow others to appreciate what your mentee can now bring to the table, as well as provide more opportunities to apply those new skills.

STEP 7

# Step 8

# Promote Influence Skills

*"Who shall set a limit to the influence of a human being?"*

*–Ralph Waldo Emerson*

## Overview

- Recognize influence opportunities and challenges.
- Foster four crucial influence skills.
- Strengthen influence progressively.

Mari, a senior leader, was thrilled to be working with Patrick, who was slated to be developed for a senior manager role. Patrick was a product manager with an appliance manufacturer. Mari had been working with him for over a year, and they had made considerable progress with his strategic leadership and competitive insights.

Patrick had just been tapped to lead a team charged with identifying how to address the slumping sales level of their signature products. They knew customer interests were changing due to competitive products and demand for continuously enhanced features. The challenge for Patrick's team was to determine how the core products could have a variety of adaptable new elements to retain and expand their customer base. Patrick's was one of two teams charged with the same task, and he was worried about getting the funding to move their ideas forward.

STEP 8

Patrick reported to Mari that he and his team had conducted an in-depth analysis on the sales performance of two of their core products and identified customer response trends for the last 15 months. They had also researched similar products in the marketplace. After interviewing their customers and distributors, they uncovered rich insights about their customers' changing needs. Patrick understood exactly what new features would surpass their competition. He had asked Mari to help with the next steps of taking this to the finish line so the new designs could get into the marketplace within six months. "Mari, I grew up as a design engineer. My skills are growing, but what do I know really about corporate decision making?"

Mari had to check her desire to jump in and resolve Patrick's problem. She wanted to facilitate rather than simply give him her preferred solutions. During mentoring, he had made such great progress in other competencies; now it would all be put to a test.

What would you advise that Mari do? What would *you* do? We will unfold the possibilities through this chapter.

Whether your mentee is a product manager, stock analyst, trainer, social media manager, or software engineer, they will need to gain influence to get their job done successfully . . . we all do. This can be especially important after your mentee has gained skills from the mentoring and you want to boldly challenge them to apply those skills more broadly. As their mentor, you have gotten to know them, helped them understand their internal drivers, and built a trusted relationship with them. You are in the best possible position to promote influence skills. It is the next natural step in expanding your mentee's growth, and another component that will make your mentoring masterful.

In a world of interconnectedness, every significant project, every important decision, and every operational change requires your mentee to influence others. For many mentees, in their day-to-day interactions, their points of influence are already in place and working well. But how is influence achieved when mentees take risks and broaden themselves, reach out to new connections, face new obstacles, and take on a more strategic focus? Seasoned mentors love this challenge; it can take their mentees to the next level of success, focusing on a number of important skills: becoming highly effective at interpersonal relationships, building credibility, communicating effectively, becoming a trusted partner, and more.

**POINTER**

In a world of interconnectedness, every significant project, every important decision, and every operational change requires your mentee to influence others.

To influence is to have an effect on the decisions, direction, drive, and actions of others. I would add that to influence well, this needs to be done ethically and with the best of intentions. When influence is used effectively, your mentee does not need to rely on authority or power to get work done through others. In effect, you are demonstrating influence in this very process with your mentee. Influence is a useful tool to add to their skill set, and can be used in whatever role they take for the balance of their career.

## Recognize Influence Opportunities and Challenges

Early in their mentoring, still as an individual contributor, Patrick told Mari, "I'm beyond frustrated. For two weeks, I've been pitching the idea to my manager that we need a cross-function team to address the issues uncovered by customer analytics, and it's gotten nowhere. Yesterday, Roger made a similar recommendation, and the two of them are already working on the plans." Mari thought about this, and at the time, figured it was a 50–50 chance that the boss was playing favorites (as Patrick assumed); or it might just be that Patrick needed to learn about influencing.

All too often, when successful in typical interactions, people believe they are doing a good job of influencing. It is when they are out of their element, however, that they really get tested. Unaware of their need to influence differently, mentees may view the obstacles as external and out of their control.

STEP 8

Here are a few telling signs that your mentee needs to increase their influence capabilities:

- feels their ideas are overlooked, even after repeated attempts
- expects logic and facts to sell their project, action, or idea
- pressures others with demands
- reports a weak relationship with customers
- does not value growing their network
- believes that getting results are best accomplished "by the book"
- expects to get an immediate response to requests.

Look for a repeated pattern. If you see a trend, as Mari did, initiate a conversation by asking about your mentee's style of influence to get things accomplished with others. Gear your questions to raise insight from the inside out (Guiding Principle #6: Explore the internal world as a driver for external actions), helping them see that their preferred manner of influence is not the only, or necessarily the best, way. Help them understand that by trying new approaches, they may gain a handle on things they thought were circumstantial and out of their control. Use the sample questions in Tool 8-1 with your mentee to start the discussion about the need to influence.

Given Patrick's current situation, managing his team to make product breakthroughs, Mari used a set of questions to help him identify that he preferred to influence by having the data and charts do the talking. When she asked how he would get the marketing team on board with his product enhancements, he was stumped. "Well, they usually like a bit of a psychological angle with the end customer, but I'm not sure how to get that across," Patrick admitted. Realizing he did not have a good answer, the discussion left him feeling panicked and wanting to learn more. If he expected this current project to be a successful step on his path to senior management, he would need to increase his influence, and bridge from his own approach to those of the decision makers and stakeholders.

**POINTER**

Unaware of their need to influence differently, mentees may view the obstacles as external and out of their control.

STEP 8

# TOOL 8-1
## QUESTIONS TO START THE CONVERSATION ABOUT INFLUENCE

- What do you value most when others, such as peers, are asking for your buy-in or to take action on their behalf?
- Can you provide an example of how you influenced someone on something important to you in the last month?
- How do you identify who should be influenced by you?
- Do you use the same approach for each person or team you are influencing?
- What, typically, are your expectations for influencing another?
- What do you find are varying ways that people are influenced?
- How do you want others to feel as a result of your influencing conversations?
- What does your style of influence tell you about yourself?

# Foster Four Influence Skills

It wasn't long ago that influencing others translated to exerting pressure, winning, and persuasion tactics. In fact, lots of "how-to" books were written on the subject, especially oriented to negotiations and sales. Influencing others definitely had an "I" centric connotation—getting what I want and getting it my way. However, that type of approach is extremely short lived. Without direct power over that person, how could you go back to those same people and expect them to cooperate a second time or a third?

Today, the benchmark is using a positive approach that is open, honest, and collaborative—no demands or unfair coercion. Your mentee can think of it this way: Would they be willing to fully share with their leaders, spouses, or even their parents, the steps they were using to gain influence? If they're reluctant to tell the whole story because tactics were manipulative or less than honest, then something needs to change.

Mentees and mentors alike require an array of approaches for influencing, given the variety of people and situations. As shown in Figure 8-1, there are four types of capabilities that can fill your mentee's influence portfolio.

## FIGURE 8-1
## FOUR SKILLS THAT INCREASE YOUR MENTEE'S INFLUENCE

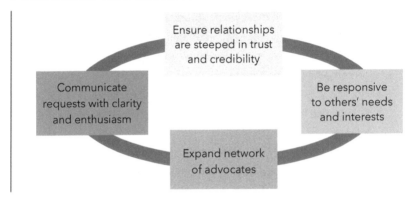

## Ensure Relationships Are Steeped in Trust and Credibility

To succeed in influencing others, especially regarding something significant, your mentee should not start that influence at the moment they make the request or proposal. The process of influence is deep seated and relies on a sound relationship already in place. Your mentee has a multitude of relationships with bosses, peers, customers, and stakeholders, and each has a different vested interest in their relationship with your mentee. To establish trustworthiness and credibility, help your mentee:

- **Communicate openly, honestly, and discreetly.** In this case, your mentee states their ideas, discloses their viewpoints, and has no secrets. They also know boundaries and keep confidential information private, so others are willing to share concerns and seek their input. There is a mutual respect between the mentee and those with whom they work. For example, if they give their word to provide feedback about how something is working, others can count on hearing back from them with the complete picture.
- **Take actions consistently and with good results.** Your mentee is reliable for getting the job done and follows through on promises made. They faithfully walk the talk. So when they make a request of a colleague, the colleague knows time spent

supporting the mentee will be put to good use. Influence diminishes, and trust can be broken if the mentee fails to meet expectations. If this is the case with your mentee, they will have some repair work to do with that colleague (discuss the disconnect with the other person and talk about what will be needed or demonstrated to restore trust).

- **Make expertise visible.** Your mentee builds credibility by showing they know their job well. They demonstrate they have learned from experience and are prepared for a conversation on the subject at any time. When asked about something they do not know, they are honest about that, and use their resources to find the answer. Then, when working to influence a project team in a certain direction, the team is more confident that the mentee is ready and able to take things to the finish line.

Mari knows that Patrick's reputation has been golden. He is viewed as a very talented design engineer, willing to find the best solutions, share his ideas, and follow through on the long list of actions to move the research and design forward. Mari feels certain he has this part of the equation—relationships steeped in trust and credibility—nailed down.

## Be Responsive to Others' Needs and Interests

STEP 8

If you had only a single opening in your busy week to give discretionary action to one of two colleagues, what would make you give to one over the other? There are probably a few factors, such as the nature of your relationship, whether one has done the same for you in the past, and even if you felt there could be damage done between you by not following through. One thing for sure: Over time, the person who has done the most for you will likely get the most from you. Called the "rule of reciprocity" by Alan Cohen and David Bradford, longtime experts in the field of influence, this type of exchange is at the heart in the majority of influence interactions (Cohen and Bradford 2017).

- **Get to know what is important to others.** No one wants to give discretionary effort to a person who is interested in only their own goals; working together should be a mutual endeavor, with both parties understanding what the other is hoping to accomplish. That requires your mentee to listen, observe, and be nonjudgmental about viewpoints that are different from their own. For example, when influencing senior executives, your mentee needs to demonstrate an understanding of long-range goals. Similarly, the operations manager wants your mentee to consider the work flow and equipment challenges.

- **Offer to help—no strings attached.** If your mentee wants others to take action on their behalf, they should certainly be doing the same. Your mentee can start that cycle by being helpful to others. So, if your mentee's colleague is stumped by a problem with a client, the mentee could sit down and brainstorm with them. Next time your mentee is struggling with a deadline, that same colleague might be the first one to help. When reciprocity really flows, we do not have a feeling of obligation; we are not thinking, "Well, he did that for me, guess now I have to do this for him." At its best, we reciprocate because we feel valued by that person.

- **Be influenceable!** One of the core concepts from two other leading influence experts, Mark Goulston and John Ullmen, is to be influenceable. They explain that this is not giving in, giving up, or lacking commitment to your principles and excellent results. Being influenceable means your mentee goes into conversations willing to believe that they may be partially or totally wrong; that the other person may be partially or completely right; and that something valuable can be learned from the interaction. In the end, once others view your mentee as open and willing to bring in others' viewpoints, there can be a meeting of the minds (Goulston and Ullmen 2013).

In this category of "responsive to others' needs and interests," Mari helped Patrick see he was not doing so well. To begin, he had a narrow range of targeted advocates that included customers, operations, and his team. He seemed disinterested in the functions that he deemed less important, such as marketing, purchasing, and even the top executive team. They did not feel valued by him. He rarely gave people in those functions the time of day; but now, he was going to need their help to move the project forward. Mari and Patrick discussed how he could start interacting with them—really listening to their needs and interests, suspending his judgment, and figuring out ways that his team's ideas could be influenced by these other teams.

**POINTER**

If your mentee wants others to take action on their behalf, they should certainly be doing the same. Your mentee can start that cycle by being helpful to others.

## Expand Network of Advocates

Think for a moment about a person you know who has significant and positive influence not based on authority. Others are willing to be persuaded, encouraged, and inspired by this person. Does it seem they have a lot of folks around them who are willing to be engaged in conversation? Your answer is probably "yes," which should not come as a surprise. The best of those who influence others build a cadre of advocates.

Mentees do not necessarily need to be people persons. They do, however, need to embody what we have talked about in this chapter—engender credibility, help others without expectation of return, listen to others and understand others' interests, communicate authentically, and provide proposals for new actions that include benefits to their stakeholders. Here is what your mentee can consider while increasing a network of advocates.

- **Build a personal board of directors.** Many mentees tend to have advocates from their own field and their immediate circle. But the further they venture out, the larger their projects, the more that circle needs to expand. Your mentee needs to think bigger to develop further. As a proponent for this approach, Lisa Barrington advises that while this personal board of directors won't ever hold a joint meeting, those individuals should provide diverse perspectives to broaden your mentee's thinking, provide feedback, and challenge them in new directions (Barrington 2018). Your mentee can identify a short list of people to get to know better: those in their discipline with a broader scope of responsibility, those who are good at influencing, and current stakeholders who do not yet know them well.

- **Prepare to make the connection.** As your mentee identifies those to add to their network, it is wise to identify a reason to connect that works for each of them. The easiest connections will be with people they already know and want to know better. For example, for people serving on a project team from another department, the reason to connect will be that shared project. For others who do not know your mentee, it makes sense that there is a mutual introduction from someone (a manager, a colleague, or yourself), along with a purpose to connect that is beneficial for both. Your mentee can ask for 20 minutes; not so much time to schedule, yet still enough time to have a substantive conversation. If the other person does not want to meet with your mentee right away, help your mentee view that as a part of the process, and to not take it personally. Managing this disappointment is part of building resilience—also important in gaining influence skills. Your mentee can either try contacting that person again highlighting the purpose, or simply move to the next person on the list.

- **Make the connection meaningful (built to last).** With a purpose in mind, your mentee meets with the potential advocate. They could be asking the other's perspectives on business, asking about experience in executing a certain program, and suggesting ways to support them. To help boost confidence, your mentee may write out a script for the conversation in advance of the meeting—not to memorize, but more as a talking aid and a motivator to actually have the meeting. They should also know that a one-time meeting is not enough; periodic follow-ups keep the connection alive, such as providing the contact with something of value (an article referencing a topic they discussed) or a simple update about how they used the advice.

For Patrick, this all seemed overwhelming at first, and frankly he wasn't that interested in making the time to do it. Mari had him prioritize who he would visit based on the needs of his team's project. Patrick turned a corner when the first person he contacted, an analyst in marketing, came through immediately with very useful data. In return, Patrick provided the analyst with a few contacts he knew in the distribution chain.

## Communicate Requests With Clarity and Enthusiasm

Importantly, your mentee's influence will also come through their words and conviction. When your mentee requires others' buy-in, budget dollars, cooperation, or specific resources, how do they get a compelling message across? Sometimes this is done in a single conversation. For larger asks, there may be multiple conversations or presentations, to the same people or to other groups.

- **Be clear about the objectives.** After laying much groundwork to build influence, at the point of communicating a request or ask, your mentee's appeal should be straightforward and transparent. Vague or half-baked communication saps momentum built up out of the starting gate. They cannot meander their way into the explanation; the purpose and benefits need to be sound. Suggest that your mentee state the headline of their request in no more than two sentences. Have them practice with you.
- **Satisfy intellect and reasoning.** Your mentee should diligently research the facts and factors that make their case compelling, whether it is a massive competitive market analysis or observations of office operations. Even with their expertise and credibility, these well-formulated and reliable facts need to be of importance through the eyes of those to

whom they are making the request. Speak to the audience's interests—whether their priorities are in long-term benefit, immediate application, cost savings, revenue generation, or staffing needs. The "ask" is made attractive based on the mutual benefit and value.

- **Engage others on an emotional level.** Communication also needs to appeal to emotions, grab the other person, be optimistic, and portray a better result or future. Your mentee's authenticity, conviction, and confidence can be magnetic. Enthusiasm lifts, inspires, and attracts followers. Stories and real examples stir others and complete the picture. But it cannot be a one-way conversation; your mentee needs to enlist others by listening and responding. As an example, a client of mine who was presenting a proposed onboarding and retention program to senior management showed all the estimated cost savings and nonfinancial benefits for the organization (that is, the logic). Then, she showed them something else: She had researched and captured the actual stories of two professionals who had recently left the company. She identified the cost of every aspect of their journeys, from recruitment to training and more. She painted a detailed picture, then summed up the associated costs and impacts for each individual case and said, "Now, let's multiply these examples by the 250 people who have left us in the last 18 months." The executives were wowed.

In the area of "communicate requests with clarity and enthusiasm," Patrick had a lot going for him. His research was comprehensive, and he certainly had his facts, figures, charts, and tables in order. In his prementoring days, that was the extent of what he did to influence management. For this effort, Mari helped him appeal to the more humanistic side—telling stories, sharing customers' excitement, showing video from focus groups. He made the meetings and presentations into a two-way dialogue, engaging stakeholders throughout the discussion, not just at the end. Mari had even suggested using humor, but he would need more practice to make that sincere. These latest presentations had the executives viewing him differently, as a more persuasive leader.

As with Mari, your conversation about influence might carry over into several meetings or become an ongoing thread during your mentoring relationship. Tool 8-2 presents questions that can help you determine your mentee's skills with the four influence capabilities.

## TOOL 8-2
### UNDERSTANDING YOUR MENTEE'S INFLUENCE SKILLS

| Influence Capabilities | Ask Your Mentee: In What Ways Do You . . . |
|---|---|
| 1. Ensure relationships are steeped in trust and credibility. | • Communicate openly, honestly, and freely<br>• Build credibility by consistently taking actions that get good results<br>• Make your expertise visible |
| 2. Respond to others' needs and interests. | • Know what is important to those you are working with<br>• Help others with no strings attached<br>• Demonstrate openness to being influenced by others |
| 3. Expand network of advocates. | • Build a diverse set of advocates<br>• Prepare for first-time meetings with potential advocates<br>• Make connections with potential advocates meaningful and recurring |
| 4. Communicate requests with clarity and enthusiasm. | • Communicate objectives and needs clearly and succinctly<br>• Appeal to others' intellect and reasoning<br>• Engage others on an emotional level |

STEP 8

## Strengthen Influence Progressively

If your mentee is working on a priority project and suddenly realizes they need to influence several people in the next two days, it may be difficult for you to help them complete that task. Strengthening influence skills is not done in a dash . . . it's more like a marathon.

Consider my sister-in-law Stephanie, a master of influence in her executive role at a West Coast hospital—and a marathon runner, with over two dozen marathons to date. Watching her over the last couple decades, I have seen her consistency and deep dedication to growing both sets of skills. While her accomplishments are visible, the behind-the-scenes work is not seen by many.

Stephanie does not simply rely on what she learned in the early days; she has increasingly added more skills to address the multitude of nuances that can arise in the race. Early on, she learned the core skills: when to take short strides, when long, and how to pace. Over time, she concentrated on more sophisticated tactics, such as focusing on the excitement of running up hills because the elevation lifts her, training in harsh weather for mental fortitude, and spreading her arms open to avoid the inevitable shoulder hunch that occurs after a few hours of running. So whether she lands in Anchorage during the rainy summer season or New York on a chilly fall day, she can be confident in her readiness for the conditions that await her. Getting to that level and breadth of expertise was certainly not a quick journey.

Just like Stephanie, your mentee needs to build muscle and multifaceted skills. Strengthening influence requires discipline and conscientiousness to build a range of approaches that work well in many situations. Tenacity, testing oneself in a variety of settings, and tracking impact produces enhanced results. Help prepare your mentee for the mix of influence circumstances they will encounter as their career expands. Consider these approaches for maximizing influence skills over a period of time:

- **Recognize that influence is an iterative process and often takes multiple rounds.** The more complex the project or request, the more people, methods, and time required. Consider the executive who wanted to make a massive overhaul to systems that were at the heart of research data management for her company. She conducted round after round of meetings, visits, and inquiries to influence a set of strategic decision makers. She hit many brick walls, but kept plugging away. She found out she needed to tailor her approach for different players and had her advocates weigh in with advice and feedback. In all, the influence process took two years and ended with the complete buy-in for the changes and implementation she recommended. Some things, your mentee just cannot rush.

**POINTER**

Strengthening influence requires discipline and conscientiousness to build a range of approaches that work well in many situations. Help prepare your mentee for the mix of influence circumstances they will encounter as their career expands.

- **Explicitly seek out influence opportunities to practice skills on a regular basis.** For example, encourage your mentee to step in when the team needs to garner attention from a line manager. By using those skills consistently, they will be ready and confident when they need to use them for the next big effort. (Stephanie says, "Never let the muscles atrophy between races, even if marathons are 10 months apart, so that you never have to build the muscle up from zero.") Anticipate what specific action will be required for each influence situation, such as getting more resources from management, recommending innovation, or making department improvements.

- **Facilitate understanding that the difficulties encountered could be with the mentee, not the others.** With each new skill, it may be necessary to go inside to learn behavior on the outside (Guiding Principle #6: Explore the internal world as a driver for external actions). For example, when Patrick first tried adding storytelling to his presentation to the executives and it went flat, he was quick to conclude that the technique was simply the wrong approach. Mari had him replay the scene to help him understand that his nervousness and lack of conviction meant he had not leveraged the story to sell his key points. This technique is tough for a numbers-driven guy. Before the next time, some rehearsal with Mari was in order.

STEP **8**

- **Track progressive results of new behaviors.** Identify what worked well and why. Consider progress relative to the four types of influence skills and underscore strengths and gaps. As your mentee progresses, look for the types of results that demonstrate increasing influence. Tool 8-3 lists sample behaviors to guide you and your mentee.
- **Anticipate setbacks and be tenacious.** There are no guarantees, and not all attempts will be successful. There will be disagreements and roadblocks. Your mentee will need to overcome others' objections or even lack of interest. Tenacity will be called for in the face of obstacles, and rerouting or trying a different method (Guiding Principle #5: Drive risk taking for new mindsets and behaviors). Each of these setbacks can be turned into lessons. Consider an example. No one in Jared's department had told him that the requests for analytics after the customer survey launched would be so overwhelming. His focus had been on the design and execution of the survey, for which he had gotten lots of positive feedback. But once department heads heard that the results were in, there were demands for slicing and dicing the data in countless ways. He even had to cancel a long weekend he had planned as a respite after completing the survey. His early excitement about the requests evolved into feeling paralyzed by the workload; then he reached out to his mentor, Isaac, in between their regular meetings. In his discussion with Isaac, he identified how he could both prioritize and put boundaries on how requests would be handled. Though it was a painful lesson, he learned that these projects have multiple finish lines, and to plan for all of them at the front end, not as they occurred.

## Tool 8-3
## Proof That Influence Skills Are Increasing

- Mentee understands and incorporates the needs and ideas of others into the plan.
- Mutual give-and-take is apparent in mentee's mutual discussions and actions.
- Others are enthusiastic about working with mentee when asked.
- There is increasing interest in mentee's vision of the project and its potential impacts.
- Mentee's network of advocates throughout the organization has increased.
- More people are now seeking mentee's counsel and support.
- Mentee's work and ability to manage changes are progressing positively; no drama.
- Mentee's requests or proposals are clear, compelling, and engaging.
- Mentee is asked to be part of more wide-reaching decisions.

Turning back to our main story, in the end, Patrick benefitted greatly from having Mari guide him through building his influence skills. For a high-performing professional who believed doing excellent research and thoughtful work would get him ahead, it was eye opening and time consuming to see just how much influencing encompassed: building relationships, gaining credibility, garnering goodwill through good deeds, and broadening his communication approach. Yet, these skills will serve Patrick in many ways—not just for influencing the results of his product enhancement project. These skills have also enhanced his ability to work collaboratively across the organization, deepened his appreciation of executive management's perspective, and increased his positive career trajectory.

You can do the same for your mentee. With the skill development in other areas they have garnered from your mentoring, advancing their influence skills will be the next essential element to propel their career.

STEP 8

## The Next Step

The last five chapters have explored how you can advance and perfect the skills of your mentee, capping it off with greater ability to influence. Next, we'll look at how you can advance and perfect your skills, handling the stickiest of situations that can otherwise frustrate and immobilize mentors. Learn more about addressing the challenges mentors face in step 9.

# Step 9

# Address Mentor Challenges

*"If you aren't in over your head, how do you know how tall you are?"*

*–T. S. Eliot*

## Overview

- Neutralize four mentoring relationship roadblocks.
- Succeed with mentees who are challenging.
- Manage outside influencers.

Imagine a place where you could get abundant insights from mentors' experiences as their progressive months of mentoring unfold. Such a place exists with a mentors' peer cohort. These groups are established for the mutual learning and support of mentors. Mentors might meet monthly, for example, to discuss successes, share resources, and, inevitably, spend the majority of the time working through their current mentoring challenges.

In observing and leading such groups, I have learned that more experienced mentors often anticipate some twists and turns in the mentoring relationship, and push forward. Newer mentors encounter these as surprises. What started out as a friendly collaboration with glowing anticipation evolves into . . . something else. The mentors feel disappointed, worried, mystified, angry, or taken for

More experienced
mentors anticipate
twists and turns in
the mentoring rela-
tionship and push
forward, while newer
mentors encounter
them as surprises.
Mentors should see
these challenges
not as impenetrable
barriers but as big
turning points in the
mentoring process.

granted. Occasionally a mentor quits mid-course. I even had one mentor tell me that based on the experience with her mentee, she would never mentor again.

That's a shame. With a different mindset, mentors can see these challenges not as impenetrable barriers but as big turning points in the mentoring process when they can learn a great deal about themselves. It is a delight to be a mentor when things run smoothly; it is a real test of our mentoring when we face the challenges and take them on. Your role can be demanding, which is all the more reason you will experience great satisfaction from overcoming mentor obstacles.

## Neutralize Four Mentoring Relationship Roadblocks

Several roadblocks can occur regularly and organically within the mentoring relationship. You are likely to encounter one or more of them as you continue to mentor others. In Elaine's case, she was uncomfortable with her mentee's style of presenting himself. Brad would often wear a stylish sports jacket and patterned ("wild," according to Elaine) socks, and had an entire wardrobe of glasses in various colors to match his outfits. She deemed this less than professional; but what bothered her much more was the realization that she was judging him for expressing himself. Whether it was his behavior or her own biases, she was having trouble really connecting with him.

Roadblocks such as these needn't be any more than a temporary situation, and it is good to catch them early. Before your next meeting, take stock of how the relationship has been going, using questions like the ones in Tool 9-1.

STEP **9**

# Tool 9-1

## Taking Stock of the Mentoring Relationship

Within our relationship, how would I describe . . .
- Evidence that our relationship has deepened with time?
- Whether I am feeling disconnected from my mentee?
- That we have established a conversational safety space?
- My mentee's willingness to share stories about feeling disappointed, uncomfortable, or frustrated?
- How my mentee is making steady progress against goals?
- Indication that my mentee's progress seems stalled?
- Evidence that my mentee feels respected, supported, and encouraged?
- How I feel after meetings with my mentee—satisfied, frustrated, grateful, flat?

If your answers to any of these questions have you wondering whether there are some typical roadblocks in the way of a high-functioning relationship, it's time to check it out and together address them. Be prepared to take the lead (Guiding Principle #7: Bring your best self). Let's explore four typical mentoring relationship roadblocks shown here in Figure 9-1.

# Figure 9-1

## Neutralize Four Mentoring Relationship Roadblocks

STEP 9

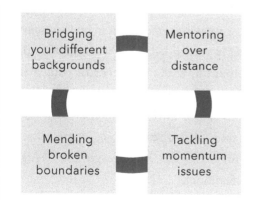

## Bridging Your Different Backgrounds

During the initial phase of your relationship, the delight of uncovering how much you have in common sometimes obscures the need to bridge to one another's values, mindsets, or work habits. If you experience a disconnect or believe your mentee is experiencing this, you might be right on target. Be aware that your own views and ways of operating are bound to be different from your mentee's. In fact, from their perspective, you may be the person who is out of step. For example, while you believe they are not serious enough about their work ethic and want to address that with them, they may be thinking your approach to work life is outmoded.

Types of differences that can create a barrier include cultural background; generational (including the mentee being the older person); sexual orientation; religious, especially if one of you is very observant, no matter your religion; and race. Any one of these differences can prime your mentee to feel misunderstood. Lois Zachery, mentoring guru, provides helpful ideas on the subject of "considering context" (Zachery 2012); she contends that we never operate in just one context. In effect, bridging to one another is almost always required.

Here are approaches to help bridge these differences.

## Use Self-Examination and Reflection

Do a mental check. Are you on guard, reserved, asking less probing questions than usual, or afraid you might insult your mentee? Where are your biases? Have you made assumptions that are misplaced? Take time to notice and understand what you are feeling and thinking. Dig deep. After all, most of us grow up with some biases in our households, and those biases may be deeply embedded. This is a growth opportunity for you. Learn more about how the difference of your mentee makes you uncomfortable. Identify stereotypes you hold that need to be addressed, bringing your best self into your interactions. Elaine, mentioned earlier in this chapter, was already doing some reflecting after her first meeting with Brad and was eager to get over her own judgment of this talented professional.

## Appreciate Differences

When the conversation turns in the direction of differences, use that as a chance to lean into it. Ask simple and relevant questions to learn more. For example, if your mentee describes their upbringing in a religiously strict household, you might ask with interest, "Can you describe how that has impacted you as a professional?" or, "How have those values made a difference in your life?" Listen sincerely, reserve your judgment, and appreciate their life experience. For example, Elaine ended up asking Brad how his personal style was an asset to him at work. When he explained that people identified him as a "creative" and consulted with him on matters of innovation and creativity, she began to consider how she presented herself (that is, "conventional") and the impact it had on her own relationships; this awareness was powerful stuff. Now, she was leaning into the relationship more, anticipating what she could learn about him—and about herself—from getting to know him better.

**POINTER**

Seek to understand your mentee's world, not necessarily by asking direct questions, but by finding useful sources of information. Learning about their culture, religion, or age group may not tell you everything about your mentee, but it will get you closer to having an understanding.

## Be an Anthropologist

Seek to understand your mentee's world, not necessarily by asking direct questions, but by finding useful sources of information. Learning about their culture, religion, or age group may not tell you everything about your mentee, but it will get you closer to having an understanding. Given your mentee's differences, what are norms? What are priorities and values in the work world? What is most important in their life balance? As you are gleaning this information, add to that your tolerance and patience, and you will continue to make your meeting times a safe place to discuss, explore, and grow.

STEP 9

## Mentoring Over Distance

Today, as our world is brought closer by technology, mentoring long distance is not uncommon. In fact, one of my client organizations purposely sets up mentoring between individuals in different parts of the world to create greater connectivity within their company. It also primes professionals to take roles in other regions of the business. Mentoring via technology is also a great backup to local pairs who are hindered by weather or time constraints for commuting.

Why is mentoring via technology that spans distance considered a mentoring relationship challenge? Even with the visual and audio connection to one another, it is tough to pick up on nonverbal cues, changes in facial expression, nervous ticks, or quiet sighs that can be important clues as to what is going on with your mentee in the conversation. You will need to work harder to create the same level of connectedness miles and cultures away from each other; or, sadly, settle for less. You might also have other distractions in your conversational environment that can be tougher to manage (for example, background noise). As well, the difference of time zones can put you on unequal energy levels. All requires extra vigilance from both of you to create that selected environment which is quiet and private, setting the tone for a private conversation.

Here are approaches to use when mentoring long distance.

### Know Your Technology

Get comfortable with technology you both agree on, whether it is a phone application or web-based platform. Rather than hold videoconferencing as something unique, view it as essential for mentoring at a distance. Test and align technology in advance so there is no last-minute scramble. Sometimes corporate safety policy means that access to certain video applications is blocked. So plan accordingly rather than lose 20 minutes during the meeting time while you figure it out.

### Create Privacy at Both Ends

Just like you would when in person, make certain the environment at both ends of the conversation is private. For some whose mentees have open office environments, the mentees go to their car or other "hidden" area to use a video application. While your mentee may deem such privacy as unnecessary, you should push for this, as it will allow conversations to go places that could not happen if others can overhear.

### Schedule Check-Ins

Check with your mentee each meeting about how this is working out and what adjustments need to be made. This is very helpful, especially if you vary how you ask the question so it does not seem redundant. For example, you can ask, "How is this conversation going?" or "Have I missed picking up on something?"

## Tackling Momentum Issues

Just about every mentor and mentee have expectations about the pace of work getting accomplished, hoping to turn those ambitious goals into reality. Then, life happens, and goals are not met as planned. What could be hindering the momentum? Maybe you preferred to keep your conversations informal and just talk about what's on your mentee's mind. Or, your mentee has reached their interim goal (for example, secured a role on a special assignment) and now seems less engaged about the larger goal. Or, you have too much to cover in each meeting and you never get to certain items. Whatever it is, one of you in the pair feels less driven or is distracted. If it keeps going this way, you will each get less from the experience, and goals will not be achieved.

Consider these approaches to address momentum issues.

### Confirm Expectations and Goals

Are the development goals still as meaningful, or do they need to be altered to be made more engaging? After all, these are not performance goals related to the mentee's department plan. Tweaking mentoring goals along the way keeps them consistent with the mentee's changing reality and interests. Find ways to discuss the goals each meeting, directly or indirectly. For example, when your mentee describes how they handled a client conversation, relate it back to

STEP 9

their goal of becoming a trusted advisor and ask how the interaction demonstrates greater competence. Comments like this underscore the goals you are working on, and their level of response can give you a cue about whether the goal now needs tweaking.

## Review Your Meeting Process

Periodically review three items related to your mentoring meetings: structure, scope or depth, and mutual check-ins. Do you have enough structure to ensure all the important elements are covered and you are making forward progress? If not, introduce a more mutually acceptable structure. For example, confirm the items you each want to cover, or decide you will leave the last 10 minutes of the conversation for talking about next steps and progress. As long as you guide the meeting with care, structure will not take away from the closeness of the relationship. Discuss depth and scope of what you are covering ("Do we take too much time mulling things over? Have we put too many items on our agenda?"). Finally, take a pulse regularly on how the meetings and conversations are going ("Did we accomplish what we intended during this conversation? What feedback do we want to offer each other to improve our process?").

## Assess the Level of Engagement

Ask yourself how engaged you feel in this process. Is something holding you back, whether having to do with the mentee or outside commitments? If so, look for aspects of mentoring that give the most back to you and focus on those. Reflect on your responsibility and the role-modeling you want to do for this mentee, no matter the challenges you face. If you believe it has to do with the mentee, have a conversation and ask some questions that will uncover their lack of luster. This takes courage to do, especially if you believe your mentee has some concerns about you. Get past that hump to help redirect this to more success. The questions can be worded to keep it more about process than personalities. Ask: What satisfies them the most about the mentoring? What is missing? What types of actions will add more meaning to the experience and draw them in?

## Mending Broken Boundaries

Boundaries are in place to benefit both of you, as well as to maintain the integrity of the relationship. That way, you have clarity about what's on the table to discuss and what is not. You have also decided on the level of access your mentee has with you (frequency of meetings, and an offer to call if something urgent arises that could use your counsel). Yet, the nature of your relationship might be like no other relationship your mentee has, and you will get tested.

When one or both of you breaks a boundary and gets into the habit of doing so consistently, your effectiveness as a mentor and a role model diminishes. Perhaps out of sheer enjoyment of time together, you decide to do some social activities. Or, maybe you morph into offering advice on issues such as personal finances or buying a home. I had a mentee years ago who tested me often wanting "whole life" advice. Once she set up an agenda item as, "Identify the best time to have a baby." Imagine the implications of giving advice on that one—way too much influence. I know another mentor who was so responsive in an emergency, her mentee decided to call her almost every day. At first, she was generously responsive and caring; then, her mentee became overdependent and even annoying. Know when you are going out of scope and not sticking with your original role and contract.

Here are approaches to use when boundaries are broken.

### Examine Your Own Intrinsic Rewards

Since the keeper of the boundaries often is you, if the boundary infringement continues, ask yourself how you are benefitting from the breach. Perhaps you want to come off as a nice person and don't want to let your mentee down. Or, you may find they remind you of a relative, perhaps a daughter or son, and you relish all their accomplishments at work and their accolades—you've become the hero.

To a certain extent, you have to take your ego out of it. Avoid any social activity (with the occasional rare exception, such as attending a mentee's award ceremony). Becoming too intertwined in your relationship has some hidden deficits of overdependence and transference, leading to mentoring drama.

## Be Disciplined to Keep Conversations on Track

Mutually talking about what is going on in your lives is a great way to connect at the front end of the meeting, but it should be kept brief. When the general conversation slips into more personal and life topics at length, figure out how that connects with your mentee's goals. There may be legitimate connection for bringing up a topic like their child's nursery school, such as consideration of a job switch or a move. But if topics appear irrelevant, gently nudge the conversation back on track. After you have done this a few times, they will get the idea and get down to business. Always use goals as your golden thread running through all the conversations.

## Redirect to Other People

Your mentee may have a concern or challenge that is outside your agreement, but sees you as the one person who will really listen and provide comfort. They may even say something like, "I know this probably isn't the right thing to talk about today. . . ." When that occurs, listen with concern, and then brainstorm the appropriate people who can help. I know of a mentee who wanted to place his grandmother in a memory-care unit of a nursing home and brought this to his mentor. In a three-minute conversation, the mentor helped him identify how others could be helpful, and then they got back to business. In doing so, his mentor provided empathy and a little bit of guidance, but did not open the door to advice-giving—which could have led to weekly reports about his grandmother and requests for ongoing help.

**POINTER**

Your mentee may have a concern or challenge that is outside your agreement. When that occurs, listen with concern, and then brainstorm the appropriate people who can help.

# Succeed With Mentees Who Are Challenging

One mentor's challenging mentee is another mentor's ideal learning situation. I'd like to think there are very few mentees who truly are not a candidate for development. In fact, if a mentee has qualities that make them challenging, maybe that's why they have intuitively come to mentoring. Isn't that something you two can work on? A mentor's attribution that a mentee is uncoachable may have to do more with the mentor's own tolerance and skill level.

**POINTER**

Not all mentees will be someone you find likable, nor come to you free of character flaws. It may not be ideal for you, yet, you could take it on for the learning value.

Not all mentees will be someone you find likable, nor come to you free of character flaws. It may not be ideal for you, yet you could take it on for the learning value. The benefit to you could be learning more about yourself and how you respond to someone who pushes your buttons; learning to increase tolerance, patience, and compassion; and, learning various approaches to work with someone like this (you may encounter more people with your mentee's characteristics). Be courageous and lean into working with this person when others will not.

As an example, Ronald thought his mentee Ava constantly stretched the truth (or lied altogether), such as when she talked about why her manager reassigned her or what caused her to miss deadlines. When Ronald asked questions to validate his unspoken hypotheses that she was dishonest, Ava's responses always covered her tracks. He could see the pattern; nonetheless, she artfully found a way to avoid answering certain questions where (he thought) she could be found out. Dishonesty was a trigger for Ronald; he was angry about it, obsessed over it, and thought he might end the mentoring early.

When mentors encounter attributes of their mentees they find challenging, how can they overcome the situation and still make progress? Let's take a look at several types of mentee characteristics that can test a mentor's tolerance and how those could be approached.

STEP **9**

## Lack of Honesty

People usually lie because they believe the truth will be unacceptable to the other party, and the other person will think less of them. What they may not realize is that just the opposite is happening. If you find your mentee has lied or you suspect it, as Ronald does, check out the following:

- Assess the level of trust within the relationship. Is it safe enough for your mentee to open up, or do they feel you are going to judge what they say?

- Be patient. Allow them to hang onto their misrepresentation and take it as their truth. Do not dwell; instead, move on to other topics and allow them to feel acceptable to you. Your mentee may or may not ever correct the former misdeed, but going forward, may end up being more honest. As they get into a pattern of being more open with you, they can transfer that authenticity to their work situation.

- When the time seems right and your mentee has been more transparent with you, carefully ask about what they find less than acceptable about themselves. Ask how they believe others view that characteristic: "When an individual is ____ (fill in with the less-than-acceptable characteristic just mentioned), what do you think is the impact on others?" "What could improve that relationship with others?" Explore what they believe is the effect of lack of candor with others and what it will take to overcome that—which may be quite challenging for your mentee to do.

## Rudeness or Arrogance

When a person dismisses others' input, acts distant or superior, or believes their answer is always "the" answer, there is definitely an issue with their interpersonal skills. If your mentee acts in this manner, unless they are as brilliant and successful as Steve Jobs (or perhaps even despite that), their career will be hampered. No matter how smart and productive, the mentee is going to turn off others, and eventually people will limit their interactions with them, causing them to be less effective. What could be behind the behavior? According to research on arrogance and how to address it (Lombardo 2009), the mentee may be acting defensively to avoid getting too close to others, or be too impatient to interact with anyone not in their smart peer group. They may not even outwardly care that they turn others off.

This is a case for increasing emotional intelligence (Guiding Principle #6: Explore the internal world as a driver of external actions). Work with your mentee to help them appreciate the short- and long-term implications of their behavior. No need to label them as "rude" or "arrogant"; just be descriptive of the behavior itself ("When you often have the right answer and cut others off, it has the effect of . . ."). If they understand the impact of their behavior and are motivated to make improvements, you have already helped them develop considerably. Have them take into account how they want others to feel as a result of an interaction with them. Have them observe how a peer or manager who is both smart and values others handles interactions. They might also speak with that person to ask how to cope when the input is not up to par. Then, suggest they set up some fieldwork to try new interpersonally focused behaviors and observe others' responses. And, as a reminder, content in step 5 serves as a resource on increasing emotional intelligence with your mentee.

**POINTER**

Work with your mentee to help them appreciate the short- and long-term implications of their behavior. No need to label them as "rude" or "arrogant"; just be descriptive of the behavior itself. If they understand the impact of their behavior and are motivated to make improvements, you have already helped them develop considerably.

STEP 9

## Low Ethics

Consider a mentee who disregards the rules, appears self-serving, or constantly finds loopholes within directives and expectations. This is typically not the person with whom you want to work. Yet, the bigger picture reveals that they are creative, productive, and skilled in a number of areas. As an example, I remember Derrick, a professional I had gotten to know in a company I consulted with. One day he told me he had well-developed plans for a new business. I asked if he was leaving his job. He responded, "No, I have created a lot of efficiencies with my current role, and can now get all my work tasks done in about 20 hours a week. I keep my head down, and no one seems to notice what else I'm busy with. So, I will be working my new business right here from the office." I was quite surprised at his attitude toward his employer (and that he actually shared this with me!). Derrick was viewed by some managers as exceptionally bright, charming, creative, and productive; but now I realized he was no role model for his company and its values.

The degree of indiscretion can guide your approach. Sometimes low ethics are situational, perhaps where your mentee has noticed others acting in the same way (for example, taking office supplies home for their own use). For these mentees, well-worded questions, carefully delivered, will raise awareness ("What is this behavior getting you? What is this behavior costing you? What value does this bring for you compared with the impact it has?"). Other situational incidences can be a custom brought over from another culture, which simply requires a straightforward discussion and examples of handling things according to the prevailing values.

Then there are those who "slip" when under stress and blame circumstances. The approach to set the mentee on the right course is raising both awareness and perspective. You can begin with exploratory questions ("What makes values particularly important during times of high stress? What will this require of you?"). If they are headed for leadership roles, they can be made aware of the impact of trading values for expedient results. Have a conversation that has them viewing their behavior from multiple perspectives: their manager, customers, colleagues, and the impact on them. In addition, there are a lot of articles, books, case studies, and even TED talks on this subject you can suggest.

Finally, for the worst offenders—mentees who take low ethical actions on a more regular basis—the job of raising their awareness and helping to reshape behavior can be more daunting. This a longer term situation, with the first big step getting them to care about and see the consequences. Start a conversation about demonstrating values through behaviors. How do they see this in others? In what ways are they already doing this? Where can they improve?

## Defensiveness

Many mentees, even mentors for that matter, act defensively on occasion. When it is a regular part of your mentee's communication style, it's problematic. Your mentee is viewed as unwilling to receive feedback, denying mistakes, blaming others, and rationalizing failures. Others find the mentee difficult to speak with and become guarded and limited in discussions with them, fearful of setting them off. It affects their one-on-one relationships, and they can also become the spoiled apple in a barrel, disrupting their entire team dynamic. What can be at the crux of their behavior?

Defensiveness is an act of self-protection. Often unconscious, it is an attempt to conceal feelings of shame and insecurity, even from themselves. The roots of defensiveness may have started in their childhood. They do not want to be seen in a negative light and will say almost anything to avoid it. In terms of brain chemistry, they become flooded with cortisol, which leads to the "fight-or-flight" response and shuts down reasoning.

The most important attribute in your approach to this mentee is to provide safety. When they feel understood and respected by you, they will be able to open up and explore their responses, behaviors, and impact. When you speak with them, let them know you are on their side and truly value them. Very likely, they see their own behavior and want it to be different, but cannot get a handle on it. Help them tune inward when these incidences occur, become aware that they have been triggered, and calm themselves from the perceived threat (often a deep breath gives a couple seconds to clear the mind). Then, they can reengage in the conversation more constructively.

At first, your mentee may have to force themselves into a more congenial discourse. With practice, they will learn how they get triggered

STEP **9**

and how to calm themselves, and will know that others are not really out to get them. Changes will occur over time, and self-reflection will be key. Your mentee can track their incidences in a journal, including what triggered them, how they felt, what happened once they took a breath, and how they were able to redirect their behavior. As they bring these reflections to upcoming meetings, you may also be able to add direct positive feedback regarding their improvements based on the conversations you two have had. Your tact, safety, and support can go a long way toward improving their interactions with others.

We have just taken a look at approaches to work with mentee who can test us. Be up for the challenge! Tool 9-2 provides insights and methods for addressing these challenges. Before jumping into action, tune in to uncover if and how you are triggered by your mentee's behavior. Take a deep breath if you are affected (many mentors are triggered by such behaviors), and then manage your conversation most effectively—as you are asking them to do.

## TOOL 9-2
### MASTERFULLY WORKING WITH MENTEES WHO ARE CHALLENGING

| The Challenge | Perspective About Mentee | Suggested Mentor Approach |
|---|---|---|
| Lack of honesty | • May believe the truth will be unacceptable to others<br>• Wants to be viewed in a positive light | • Assess the level of trust and safety the mentee is experiencing with you and take action to increase these as needed.<br>• Move to topics where they will feel supported by you rather than judged.<br>• When it appears the mentee feels open or safe (in that meeting or another conversation), explore the impact of dishonesty, without any accusation. |

STEP 9

| The Challenge | Perspective About Mentee | Suggested Mentor Approach |
|---|---|---|
| Rude or arrogant | • May believe is smarter than others and impatient to deal with someone "not at their level"<br>• May be single-minded and unaware of, or unconcerned about, impact on others | • Increase mentee's awareness of impact on others and the overall effect on their interactions.<br>• Help mentee understand that positive results are not garnered by smarts alone; a variety of skills are needed.<br>• Encourage mentee to tune inward regarding these interactions (i.e., what they are feeling just prior to encounter) so they are aware when it occurs and can correct their own behavior. |
| Low ethics | • Believes they can do better bypassing rules; stretches the boundaries of the rules<br>• Is joining others' indiscretions, which seems to make it OK<br>• May have a more deep-seated, selfish approach where personal gains justify behaviors | • Help mentee view their behaviors in the larger perspective of the organization and with a longer-term view.<br>• Ask questions to raise personal insight, reach beyond asking about rationales for behavior. Instead move to questions about how they believe others might view them.<br>• Help mentee identify why ethics matters in general and for their career. Have mentee report on incidences where they took the high road with positive results. |
| Defensive | • Is protecting self from feelings of shame or insecurity<br>• Feels threatened, wants to avoid being seen as having done something wrong | • Assess the level of trust and safety the mentee is experiencing with you and assure them you are on their side and value them.<br>• Encourage mentee to tune into incidences that trigger them, learn to calm themselves (e.g., through self-talk), remain open to the other party, and explore the content of their discussion.<br>• Ask them to log incidences when they were successful and unsuccessful during such interactions, and observe with them the trend of their improved responses over time. |

# Manage Outside Influencers

Mentees have many relationships in their lives, and some of those people will be keenly tuned into the fact that they are participating in a mentoring relationship. These people are invested in your mentee's development process for any number of reasons: being a big fan of your mentee and wanting to see them flourish; anticipating they will take the organization to higher levels of performance; or, hoping that they correct some of their work habits. They will certainly watch from the sidelines, and some will exert involvement in this development process (whether or not you and your mentee seek it).

Anticipating and managing these influencers puts your mentee in charge of the GPS, rather than having someone else call out directions from the backseat. Let's take a look at these players. In the broadest sense, these influencers can be divided into two groups: deliberate supporters and inadvertent diverters. Sometimes the very same people can end up being in both categories, and it will be up to your mentee to figure that out.

## Deliberate (Thoughtful) Supporters

Your mentee will find several people in their network of relationships who are cheerleaders for the mentoring process and supporting them to take growth even further. Their encouragement is golden throughout, and most especially when the mentee is testing new behaviors, stretching in uncomfortable ways, or encountering some rough patches in their development. Here are some types of people who may show up as deliberate supporters and how they can be useful:

- **Trusted colleagues.** Your mentee can ask for candid feedback from those who see them in action; they should be specific for the feedback requested, geared to the areas where they are working to make changes. This can be established as an ongoing request, checking in with this colleague on a regular basis. They even make this arrangement mutual, so both are giving and receiving feedback.

- **Supervisor or manager.** Unique opportunities that a manager can provide, like almost no one else, are new growth assignments to match your mentee's development interests. Your mentee can request a special project, involvement on a task force, or the opportunity to shadow someone who matches the skill they are working on. Additionally, a manager can be a source of referrals to experts as well as someone who can track progress of the mentee's increased skills.
- **Parent or sibling.** This family member can serve as a life historian as your mentee delves into the roots of their habits and examines personal values and life lessons.
- **Associates from other departments or organizations.** Your mentee may find these associates useful in providing perspective on how work and relationships are carried out in differing environments.

While you serve as the prime facilitator of growth, this constellation of supporters will be important to make the development experience more complete. You and your mentee should encourage their positive support.

## Inadvertent Diverters

It also happens that some mentoring onlookers can actually be disruptive. Their effect can be so subtle that neither of you realize it is happening. Others who are inadvertently intruding with their needs and interests can diminish your mentoring effectiveness. It could be your mentee's partner asking about whether they are working on their temper, or their manager wanting to know if they feel they are making any progress. While their inquiries can be outwardly viewed as caring gestures with the best of intentions, these diverters may not realize they are serving their own interests and not your mentee's.

In other cases, the intrusion is overt, and they may feel entitled to make a specific request, such as the mentee's department head

STEP 9

steering them to work on a specific goal. I once had a mentee whose whole team formulated questions she would bring to me in mentoring conversations, so that it helped them in the organization initiative they were executing. Because I was new to the process and relatively green, her team was getting my consulting services instead of my mentee getting my mentoring.

What is the impact of inadvertent diverters? They take the mentoring in a direction that is not part of the original plan. A detour is triggered, missing the planned avenue to growth and goals. It can also cause your mentee to shut off that source of disruption (for example, your mentee avoids talking with a work colleague) or to bring up fewer topics with you, knowing that others will be asking about what got covered in your meeting. These disruptions can also cause a break in boundaries and affect the safety of the conversations.

Both of you will need to be mindful to disruptions and call them out for what they are. Identify the risks that need to be navigated when managing the diversion. As a pair, you can decide what can be done to kindly address the disruptor yet minimize the diversion. When you shine a light on this, the disruption is minimized.

Tool 9-3 offers some background about managing inadvertent diverters and proposes sample responses your mentee can provide to that individual.

No doubt as a mentor you are bound to have many challenges. Sometimes I think it would be boring without them. This chapter looked at three categories of challenge: relationship roadblocks, succeeding with mentees who are challenging, and managing outside influencers. Which of these have you been encountering? Be tenacious and resilient in the face of these obstacles and use them to sharpen your own capabilities.

# TOOL 9-3

## MANAGING INADVERTENT DIVERTERS

| Inadvertent Diverter | Indicators of Diversion | Possible Motivation | Sample Response From Mentee |
|---|---|---|---|
| Mentee's manager | Requires mentee to regularly reschedule your meetings<br><br>Wants to know what is being covered at the mentoring meetings | Feels threatened; wants to minimize mentoring contact<br><br>Wants to be involved; feels left out | Discuss with manager; indicate mentoring will not negatively impact the relationship with the manager<br><br>Share appreciation for their interest; offer only general highlights |
| Mentoring program manager | Probes too deeply, beyond the agreement of what would be shared about progress | Feels responsible for knowing if the mentoring process is going well | Mentor thanks program manager for interest and for understanding the need to keep boundaries intact; shares only high-level highlights. |
| Mentee's significant other | Wants to steer the topics of discussion based on own interests | Views this as an opportunity to resolve personal relationship issues | Tell significant other they understand the interest in their mentoring, and they are working on their development |
| Company leader | Goes beyond original agreement; asks mentee to set specific goals | Takes ownership for what happens in the mentoring process | Share appreciation for leader's involvement in making the program happen; offer only general highlights |
| Interested colleague | Probes too deeply | Might be envious of the mentoring relationship | Let colleague know their relationship is valued, and the process works best when certain things are kept private; encourage colleague to find a mentor |

STEP 9

# The Next Step

I hope mentoring has been a most rewarding experience for you and your mentee. Though your relationship may be maintained, this focused development format with regular meetings, like all good things, will come to an end. Do not bypass the closing step; it consolidates the learning, adds greater depth to the entire experience for both of you, and potentially lays the groundwork for a continuing relationship. Bringing closure is captured in the next and final step.

# Step 10

# Consolidate Learning and Bring Closure

*"I know that all good things must come to an end and I've had an incredible ride. I just want to end it on the right note."*

*–Alonzo Mourning*

## Overview

- Anticipate closure.
- Individually prepare for the wrap-up conversation.
- Conduct the wrap-up conversation.
- Consolidate the learning from your experience.

During the Association for Talent Development's 2018 International Conference & Exposition, an ardent proponent of company mentoring programs stood up in a room of a couple hundred development professionals and asked, "Why are we talking about an end point for a mentoring relationship?" He sounded frustrated. He went on to say that he hoped all the relationships he had helped establish in his company program would go on and on. If you are feeling the same way he did, let me put your mind at ease: I am not proposing an end to the relationship (that is optional); rather, this is a completion to the structure of and focus on deliberate development.

There are numerous advantages to having an end point to the mentoring relationship; let's consider three:

 STEP 10

1. The first advantage relates to the expectation at the start of the relationship. Though some won't say this, many people do not want to sign on to a voluntary relationship with no end in sight, no matter the benefits. That original partnering, expectation setting, and planning for outcomes is much cleaner and clearer if you share an expectation of what you will be working on and how long that might take.

2. Working toward an end point puts structure and momentum into the process. It gives it a beginning, a middle, and an end to work toward. This helps keep momentum focused on ensuring goals are met.

3. Having no articulated end point makes it awkward for one of the partners to announce they want to wrap up. In fact, it may cause the closure to be painful, with either a mentor feeling taken for granted or a mentee feeling dismissed. When no closure is planned, the relationship may morph into something else, and you miss the important opportunity to review what has been accomplished and plan for next steps.

I learned a lesson about wrap-up the hard way years ago, when I responded to the request for mentoring of a bright and driven professional. We had a fairly in-depth process as I supported her through crucial career transitions. After a couple years of working together, with significant career advancements, she started postponing meetings, and then stopped communications altogether. Apparently, she had fulfilled milestones, was feeling confident in her new role, and no longer had a need for her mentor (me!). Yet, I had been invested in helping her through hard times and wanted to savor the positive results she was now seeing.

Thinking back, we had never really discussed wrap-up; I had never initiated a closure conversation, and I was left hanging. In the years since, we have exchanged the occasional email; and in her last email, she sent a company announcement for her latest big promotion and wrote, "Thank you again for the mentorship! I hope I continue to make you proud. :)" Really uplifting, for sure; yet I realize that final step of wrap-up would have taken us even further.

Though it can be mixed with emotion—something you might want to avoid—this final segment of mentoring should be illuminating, enjoyable, and gratifying. Think of it as a graduation, worthy of celebration! Consult Figure 10-1 for an overview of the wrap-up process.

## FIGURE 10-1
### THE FOUR-PART PROCESS FOR CLOSURE

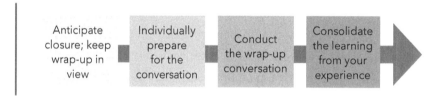

## Anticipate Closure and Keep the Wrap-Up in View

If you were developing an organizational change process that was to be presented to management in six months, you would create a plan, gather your resources, and get to work. In the early stages, you might get so wrapped up in the project launch and involving many stakeholders that you need to tweak the timeline a bit. There could be so much more you'd like to do, new questions have been raised; you wish you could cover it all. But, you recognize the importance of the deadline and work toward addressing the remaining priorities in the allowable time. Within a month or so of the deadline you would be pulling all the elements of the project together. You would have focused energy, right to the end.

The mentoring process is like that. After you are past the planning phase and into the thick of things, you can get lost in the heat of the moment, find new avenues to explore, and want to keep going. Of course, you might extend your time for a little bit. However, once the end point is identified, in the last several weeks it is important to discuss closure and plan for it.

## Identify the End Point

Perhaps when you started the mentoring, you left the end point flexible. That's OK. However, be mindful that toward the end of mentoring, mentors sometimes get caught up in the enjoyment of the relationship. They forget about the purpose of mentoring: the mentee's growth and increased confidence and independence. Be vigilant for signs that the energy is waning and goals have neared completion, even if you do not want the relationship to end. You can approach this by simply asking for an in-depth check-in on progress, and, as part of that, the two of you will look at how much mentoring is left and the best timing for wrapping up. That way, you are both part of the decision and the planning for the important final portion of the mentoring.

**POINTER**

Be vigilant for signs that the energy is waning and goals have neared completion, even if you do not want the relationship to end.

Tool 10-1 identifies the signs that it is time for a mentoring wrap-up. If you and your mentee experience two or more of these signs, open the conversation about what you would like to do next. It still may not be the right time to wrap up, and you might decide instead to rev up your process. But at least you will have the importance of doing closure well on the radar.

## TOOL 10-1
### SIGNS IT IS TIME FOR A MENTORING WRAP-UP

- You both agree that the goals of mentoring have been completed.
- There is less drive in the conversations; it is far less engaging even though there are more items to discuss.
- Your mentee has grown a good deal, and has gained confidence, self-awareness, and experience; now it is time for them to act with greater independence.
- The focus of the meetings has morphed into something else, and you are no longer working on professional development goals. For example, you may have become the

"cool parent" to them, or, occasionally, when the mentor is the younger of the two, you may end up feeling like a peer and want to be friends.

- There is a new pattern of postponing, shortening, or canceling meetings.
- There is a significant life change for one of you, such as a move to another location or a big career change.

Recall the mentoring pair of Tomás and Bernice from our discussion in step 3. Bernice wanted to work with Tomás so that she could move from being an HR policy enforcer to a trusted advisor of company leaders. Tomás really drove home the point of setting solid, ambitious, and doable goals. That was an important step for Bernice, as she got clarity on just what she needed to do. Tomás was a seasoned mentor, and Bernice got into a rhythm of formulating field-work (for trying out new behaviors) to conduct with the managers she supported in between their meetings.

At each meeting she would discuss the impact of what she tried in terms of her self-confidence, the client response, and the results that were achieved in moving that manager to think more strategically about managing the team's performance. If something did not work well in her interface with the client, she would report that to Tomás and look at possible reasons and new avenues to try. Over time, she got terrific results. Within a few months, managers were emailing her and stopping by her desk for guidance. Her work was shifting from policy enforcer and doing cleanup of employee relations issues to providing counsel in advance of crucial department actions.

Tomás was truly gratified by her level of commitment and the results she was getting. So, when Bernice asked if they could keep the mentoring going beyond the original planned end point, he agreed. Over the next couple months, things changed. Though they had set new goals, they were not nearly as urgent for Bernice. During discussions, they would go off on tangents, and there was no pressure to bring it back on track. While Bernice seemed to still be enjoying the conversations, Tomás started wondering about the purpose of the

STEP 10

meetings. When he talked it through with his mentor peer group, he realized he had kept the relationship going because it felt good to have such a successful protégé. He recognized he was going down the wrong track; it was time to wrap up the mentoring and decide in what way they might continue the relationship . . . maybe a visit every few months as a catch-up.

If you find yourself wanting to extend the time together, you might dig deep to uncover what is going on. Tool 10-2 offers some guidance.

## TOOL 10-2
### THE MENTOR'S REFLECTIVE GUIDE ABOUT EXTENDING THE MENTORING RELATIONSHIP

- What is the importance of extending the mentoring relationship?
- In what ways, other than the stated purpose of mentoring, is this relationship enriching me?
- How can the closure process be a growth experience for me?
- If we both want to stay connected, what is a productive way to continue the relationship?
- If I do not want to continue the relationship, how do I handle that conversation thoughtfully?

## Prime for Your Closing Discussion

Planning for this final step adds a great deal of value in identifying what was accomplished, sharing feedback about what stood out in your mentoring process and what the mentee has learned about themselves in this process. It certainly adds perspective as "an opportunity to share your hopes and vision for your mentoree's future, to affirm the growth you've seen, gain feedback from your mentoree on his/her experience in being in this relationship with you and to share what you have gained in the process" (ManagementMentors 2011). You will also anticipate next steps beyond mentoring, particularly on the mentee's career or development journey. Your encouragement and excitement for their next steps is something your mentee will particularly want from you. Importantly, the wrap-up also signals a change in the nature of your relationship; you are no longer working within the agreement you planned for months or years ago. The official commitment for meetings will end.

As the mentor, you take the lead on the wrap-up discussion, which may occur in one or two conversations. Keep your focus on making the wrap-up conversations realistic and positive. It is quite possible that not all expectations were met. Yet the discussion "is a blameless, no fault, reflective conversation" . . . "even when the relationship has been problematic, the conversation can be constructive" (Zachery 2012). A great deal of growth can be acquired for each of you when the relationship has been bumpy. Conversely, the experience may have far exceeded expectations. Whatever the outcomes, leave the relationship on great terms. You will forever be the mentor they had and looked to as a role model.

You will each come prepared for a rich and meaningful conversation. As you each anticipate the upcoming wrap-up, discuss and consider:

- targeting an approximate date and how many more meetings you will have
- identifying and filling development gaps in the remaining time, for instance, having conversations and trying certain behaviors that your mentee wants to learn more about, such as handling a tricky negotiation or making a certain type of presentation
- gathering feedback from others; for example, the mentee asks for observations of others on the specific behaviors they were addressing
- drafting questions you will use for that meeting that you both agree on; this includes a look at goal accomplishment as well as how you worked together

STEP **10**

- identifying areas in which you would particularly appreciate feedback
- exploring the option of keeping in touch.

## Individually Prepare for the Conversations

Your mentee can prepare by reviewing the jointly designed questions in advance and jotting down notes. For the most part, they can focus on things that occurred during the mentoring period, such as actions they took, new behaviors tried, and new mindsets adapted, all toward achieving the goals that were set. In addition, they will plan for the feedback they want to give you about how the mentoring conversations affected them. If there is unfinished business or results that were not within your joint control (for example, not getting a hoped-for promotion), that is good material to be considered for the "next steps" portion of your discussion.

Getting perspective on the changes that have occurred for the mentee over a period of time—whether six months, a year, or longer—can be complex. Tool 10-3 describes a method I often recommend. The mentee is asked to consider the usual way of handling a typical situation (such as, interactions with dissatisfied customers or taking a stand on marketing decisions) just prior to the mentoring, compared with how the mentee handles it now. Because you can never know what will occur during the course of mentoring (given available opportunities to test new behaviors, job change, or evolving goals), the particular focus of "before and after" is determined closer to the time of wrap-up. By answering these questions and looking at the differences of the two scenarios, evidence of changed behavior and mindsets becomes apparent.

Now onto the mentor's preparation. Remember Hilman and Jaqui from step 5? Hilman, the mentor, struggled with some reactions he was having toward Jaqui's behaviors and was able to do a mental check on those and then move onto a highly productive discussion with her. In subsequent meetings, they focused a good deal on Jaqui's self-awareness and impact on others.

STEP 10

# Tool 10-3
## Before-and-After Scenarios

- Mentee identifies the typical situation (e.g., "Developing IT solution project plan with client").
- Use the open space to describe details of the typical situation at two different times: before (looking backward to just prior to mentoring) and after mentoring (current).
- Summarize what has occurred and be ready for the wrap-up discussion.

**Typical situation being assessed:**

|  | Before Scenario | After (Current) Scenario |
|---|---|---|
| What was your mindset going into this situation? |  |  |
| What was your behavior in this situation? |  |  |
| What was the result of the interaction? |  |  |
| What was the impact on others involved? |  |  |
| What other evidence do you have of the impact and result (feedback, additional requests, or questions)? |  |  |
| Other comments |  |  |

While she had received feedback from her managers that she always seemed to see things only from her own perspective, no one had ever really worked with her on her emotional intelligence skills.

Hilman's work with her opened up a whole new world. She could sort out her internal feelings of self-worth driving her behaviors and leading her to make assumptions about her co-workers. Once she became more self-aware, without even thinking about it, her behaviors were changing. She became more authentic in her interactions and tuned into what others were saying and doing. Her relationships at work greatly improved.

As Hilman prepared for the wrap-up conversation, he looked at her goals and realized the ones she had originally articulated seemed less important compared with her emotional intelligence maturity. He also thought about the significant events in their conversations that were turning points for him, and all that he had learned from this sometimes-challenging relationship, and he was grateful. He prepared thoughts to share with her about her achievement of goals; how impressively she took on the challenge of increasing self-awareness; and the positive changes he had seen in her behaviors and through the stories she related. He also thought about what she could do next—not about his opinion of what she "should work on" (that was up to her), but more about keeping her development going, finding trusted colleagues to speak with, journaling, and joining area associations.

Hilman also prepared himself for potentially unexpected topics that she might bring to the meeting. He felt uneasy about her wanting to reexamine some of their more uncomfortable conversations. He got mentally set to handle this by determining he would focus on the following four actions: answering her questions authentically yet positively; ensuring there would not be any blaming; being open to another conversation if needed; and, leaving the conversation on a positive note.

In your preparation for the wrap-up conversation, look back at your meeting notes and your mentee's original goals, think about the crucial moments during the journey, and consider that along with how you view them currently. Determine the tone you will bring to the conversation and how it will shape the conversation. For example, how will it shape what you deliver if you are determined to be inspiring, supportive, grateful, and insightful?

I suggest that your preparation includes:

- Review the questions the two of you have planned for the conversation and jot down some notes.
- Determine the key messages you would like to share.
- Be prepared for disappointments or dissatisfactions, not seeing eye to eye on results, and unfinished business.
- Be optimistic, grateful, and encouraging.

**POINTER**

In your preparation for the wrap-up conversation, look back at your meeting notes and your mentee's original goals, think about the crucial moments during the journey, and consider that along with how you view them currently. Determine the tone you will bring to the conversation and how it will shape the conversation.

## Conduct the Wrap-Up Conversation

In this mentoring process, you have used the nature of your relationship and tailored conversations as the instrument for growth. You did not start where you wanted your mentee to go; you started where they were and where they wanted to go. You had to relinquish some power and solutions for them to grow. You traded in direct sharing of your expertise for their experimentation and accumulated confidence. Bravo!

Now it is time to bring this process to a close. Yes, it is possible your relationship will continue; yet the formal mentoring program, with a structured focus on regularly scheduled meetings, specific actions for the mentee, tracking of goal achievement, and looking at the dynamics within your relationship, is wrapping up. This conversation might be broken into two meetings, but rarely ever more than that. I recommend five parts to the discussion:

STEP **10**

1. Introduction to the conversation. You set the tone, identify the objectives of this conversation, review the agenda, and modify that plan.

2.  A review of mentee's accomplishments. This is a substantial part to the discussion, one that you each prepared for, potentially including them gathering feedback from others. This part of the conversation focuses on the mentee's journey; what they gained through the experience; accomplishments, especially relative to goals; how they now operate (differently); and how they see themselves as a result of the mentoring.

3.  A review of the mentoring process. This part of the conversation identifies highlights of your mentoring process and how the two of you related to each other to make it work. It is a combination of identifying the lessons learned in the underlying approach to mentoring (e.g., your use of high-gain questions or encouragement to take risks) and providing personal feedback. In advance, you may have identified where you each particularly wanted feedback. This may or may not be an emotional time, be sincere and caring.

4.  Next steps for mentee. Together you can discuss what is next for the mentee and their development. The best of such conversations are inspirational, aspirational, and motivational. Frame up elements of a "next steps" plan, or simply identify three actions to be taken. Some mentees want to take a break from this action for a while, but capture the ideas now, so they can pick up momentum when they are ready.

5.  Closing. Each of you expresses your parting words, ending this portion of your relationship on a positive note. Occasionally small gifts are given to the mentor, or exchanged. If I am unsure what my mentee might do as a closing gesture, I bring a handwritten note for my mentee.

Tool 10-4 is a sample guide you can bring to the wrap-up meeting.

# TOOL 10-4
## MENTOR'S GUIDE TO THE WRAP-UP MEETING

Introductory remarks (mentor takes lead):

- Establish objectives and tone of discussion.

Review mentee's accomplishments (mentee takes lead and mentor adds observations):

- In what ways were goals accomplished?
- What were most significant results?
- As a result of mentoring, what are changes to mindsets, behaviors, and skills?
- How would you characterize the difference this made in your work life (this conversation can use the insights gained from the "before-and-after scenario")?
- What did you learn about yourself? How are you different as a result of the mentoring?

Feedback regarding how you worked together (mentee takes lead, then mentor shares):

- What elements of the mentoring process were particularly supportive of our process?
- What were significant incidences that were most notable in our work (a turning point in the conversations or a breakthrough in the mentee's awareness)?
- What were highlights of our working together?

Next steps for mentee (mentee takes lead and mentor shares second):

- Are there unfinished accomplishments that require further attention? Discuss what could be next steps.
- Where is the mentee now in their career and development journey? What do they see next?
- Discuss potential next steps to continue on development path.

Closing (mentor takes lead):

- Where to from here, in our relationship? As appropriate (and if you are agreeable), discuss whether you would like to continue is a different format (e.g., catch-up conversations quarterly) and identify expectations for that relationship.
- Express gratitude; be specific about what you are most grateful for. Know that mentees express this differently, some with gifts and some with just a few words. Yet, your impact on them will continue for years to come.

# Consolidate the Mentor's Experience

Tomás had a complicated path to his final mentoring conversation. Though Bernice's accomplishments had been close to phenomenal, they never positioned a goal-achievement discussion, drifted into other topics, and needed to get back on track. Once past that hiccup, Tomás and Bernice eventually planned for and conducted a rich wrap-up conversation; they identified the wonderful achievements she had made, the new successes she was experiencing at work due to her proven increased capabilities and confidence, and the many positive aspects of their work together. Reflecting on his own lessons, Tomás surmised that it was affirming to use a multitude of mentoring approaches with someone so willing to really stretch herself, take risks, and be open to making mistakes. He had tried a couple approaches that he had not used before (role play and journaling), and they were met with great success. He recognized that his enjoyment of how much Bernice was accomplishing and admired him had blinded him to conduct a proper process of wrap-up conversation and reestablishing the relationship anew.

With regard to Hilman, at the close of his mentoring with Jaqui he recognized this mentoring had really tested his skills. He needed to overcome some frustrations and modify his expectations for outcomes. Oddly, he felt he grew more from this mentoring relationship than from many others in the past. He debriefed his experience with a mentor colleague and identified his greatest lessons as awareness that he was triggered by Jaqui's behaviors; that he could redirect his energy to make a positive impact even though he had been feeling angry; and the importance of adjusting to Jaqui's pace of achieving self-awareness. He recognized that his early disappointments had more to do with his expectations rather than Jaqui doing anything wrong. In all, he appreciated a number of newfound insights; these would stick with him for all his upcoming years of mentoring.

Though you have had your last meeting in this mentoring relationship, complete your experience by more consolidation of your learning and next steps for yourself. Have a conversation with a fellow colleague, a mentors' peer group, or someone supportive of your mentoring. Identify your biggest takeaways as a mentor, your surprises, and what you might want to do next as a mentor. Tool 10-5 suggests some questions; feel free to add your own.

## TOOL 10-5
### QUESTIONS TO CONSOLIDATE YOUR LEARNING FROM THE MENTORING EXPERIENCE

- What were my top achievements in this mentoring relationship?
- In what ways did I accomplish my personal goals for this mentoring?
- What were the results of some new approaches I used?
- What surprises did I experience? What does that tell me about my expectations?
- How did my mentoring skills stack up? What were my strengths? What were areas for improvement?
- What was most memorable about the experience?
- How do I see myself differently as a result of this experience?
- What would I look for in my next mentoring experience?
- What are ways, other than mentoring, I can use what I learned through this mentoring relationship?

# Relish Your Accomplishment and Know There Is More

Through the creation of an enriching relationship and a dedicated focus on development, you have greatly enhanced the work life of your mentee. You can already anticipate the difference mentoring is making for your mentee, whether it meant building new complex competencies, gaining greater self-awareness and perspective, or confidently taking on new career directions. You have sparked insight, reframed mindsets, challenged the status quo, and shared history with someone newer in your discipline. Your mentee will take what you have given forward, so that it is used years after your work together. You have given new life to knowledge and wisdom accrued

STEP 10

over many years. This is your legacy. The impact does not stop there; you have also grown as a result, expanding your insights, wisdom, and skills.

This book was never intended to be a "one and done." Each new mentoring relationship provides additional opportunities for your learning and a return to the book. You have shared your hopes for the future of your mentee; now consider what you see for yourself. As I express much gratitude to you for the work you have done, I also encourage you to continue on this incredible journey of masterful mentoring.

# Acknowledgments

Mentoring is a relationship-based endeavor. It is the quality of those relationships that particularly adds to its riches. Substantial relationships with a community of like-minded and experienced peers have activated us to create, shape, and implement mentoring programs and protocols. They have been spirited, innovative, and driven to ensure the mentoring work we did was of the highest caliber. From the Philadelphia Society of People and Strategy Mentoring Program, my trusted colleagues and mentoring friends include Mary Mavis, Fredy Jo Grafman, Terry Rothermel, Jim Van Horn, Doug Hilton, Erica Freedman, Lisa Duff, Gene Carroll, April Whitehead, Mark Spool, Katina Sawyer, Marcy Illich, Raymond Lee, Mary Vila, Richard Marcus, and others. Thank you for encouraging the writing of this book to show how deep attention to the mentoring process results in the most remarkable outcomes.

Few have allowed me to learn more about mentoring than the exceptional professionals who were my mentees over the last couple decades. They were willing to experiment and take ambitious actions, while also providing me with ideas and feedback. They have honored me by staying connected and allowing me to see how their lives have unfolded, including making career changes, getting married, taking big geographic moves, building families, and assuming creative and bold endeavors. Today, many are my peers, and I am grateful. While I thank all my mentees, several stand out as advancing my growth as a mentor, including Sara Rosin, Suzanne Kelso, Lori Zukin, Laura Robinson, Reena Mueller, Paula Sharkey, Paul Melniczek, and Aquin Houston.

If one's wealth is assessed by the people who surround you, my life is filled with abundance. I am most appreciative of Bev Kaye, an icon in the field of talent management, for writing the foreword to this book. She is a gracious model of generosity. Those who backed the writing of this book, reviewing drafts and brainstorming ideas, include Diana Whitney, Christy Macchione, Fredy Jo Grafman, Barb Kryger, and Elaine Biech. As well family members and friends who cheered me on and understood my lack of availability include Elaine, Robbie, Charlotte, Mark, Paul, Andrea, Kalman, Stephanie, Barb, Jerry, Beth, Lynn, Mary Jean, Ilene, Lynne, and Mia.

The team at ATD are the unsung heroes of the talent development profession. We count on them to inspire and inform us regularly about the newest and most effective ways to develop others, yet their names rarely appear on the cover of a book. I am indebted to ATD for asking me to write this book and giving me license to present this development-centered brand of masterful mentoring. They have labored to make the book just right for you, our readers. Many thanks to Eliza Blanchard, Jack Harlow, Melissa Jones, and Courtney Cornelius.

A special thank you to Dr. Judith Glaser, in memoriam, who was and continues to be a shining light in my development journey. Her pioneering work in neuroscience and Conversational Intelligence is changing the world for the better. I was enrolled in an executive coaches' certification program with her and WBECS (World Business & Executive Coach Summit) during the writing of this book, and in many ways she was a mentor to me.

Finally my sons, Jake Johanson and Aaron Johanson, are endlessly supportive. They also demonstrate considerable trust and respect for me by seeking my counsel. The deepest source of my forward journey is my husband, Dr. Andrew Johanson. Andy is my counselor, my confidant, and my muse; just about everything I do is better on account of him.

# References

ATD. 2017. *Mentoring Matters: Developing Talent With Formal Mentoring Programs*. Alexandria, VA: ATD.

Axelrod, W. 2012. "Make Your Mentoring Program Memorable." *People & Strategy* 35(4): 48-50.

Axelrod, W. 2015. "How Exceptional Manangers Use Everyday Psychology to Develop Their People." *Industrial and Commercial Training* 47(3): 121-126.

Axelrod, W., and J. Coyle. 2011. *Make Talent Your Business: How Exceptional Managers Develop Their People While Getting Results*. San Francisco: Berrett-Koehler.

Barrington, L. 2018. "Everyone Needs a Personal Board of Directors." *Forbes*, February 20. www.forbes.com/sites/forbescoachescouncil/2018/02/20/everyone-needs-a-personal-board-of-directors/#37f3f63e2bbc.

Bersin, J. 2015. "Purpose at Work: It Comes From Within." *Huffington Post*, November15. www.huffingtonpost.com/josh-bersin/purpose-at-work-it-comes_b_8567042.html.

Burkus, D. 2017. "Work Friends Make Us More Productive (Except When They Stress Us Out)." *Harvard Business Review*, May 26. https://hbr.org/2017/05/work-friends-make-us-more-productive-except-when-they-stress-us-out.

Cohen, A., and D. Bradford. 2017. *Influence Without Authority*, 2nd ed. Hoboken, NJ: Wiley.

DeSteno, D. 2016. "To Make a Team More Effective, Find Their Commonalities." *Harvard Business Review*, December 12. https://hbr.org/2016/12/to-make-a-team-more-effective-find-their-commonalities.

Glaser, J.E. 2014. *Conversational Intelligence: How Great Leaders Build Trust to Get Extraordinary Results*. New York: Bibliomotion.

Goldhill, O. 2016. "The Concept of Different Learning Styles Is One of Neuroscience's Greatest Myths." *Quartz*, January 3. https://qz.com/585143/the-concept-of-different-learning-styles-is-one-of-the-greatest-neuroscience-myths.

Goleman, D. 1995. *Emotional Intelligence: Why It Can Matter More Than IQ*. New York: Bantum Books.

Goodrich, R.E. 2017. *Slaying Dragons: Quotes, Poetry, & a Few Short Stories for Every Day of the Year*.

Goulston, M., and J. Ullmen. 2013. "To Influence, Be Influenceable." *The CEO Magazine,* May 16. http://media.the-ceo-magazine.com/guest/influence-be-influenceable.

Kandel, E.R. 2012. *Principles of Neural Science,* 5th ed. New York: McGraw-Hill Education.

Kolb, D.A., and B. Yeganeh. 2011. "Deliberate Experiential Learning: Mastering the Art of Learning from Experience." Whitepaper. Cleveland, OH: Case Western Reserve University.

Lombardo, M. 2009. *FYI: For Your Improvement - For Learners, Managers, Mentors, and Feedback Givers,* 5th ed. Lominger International.

ManagementMentors. 2011. "Saying Goodbye in Mentoring." Blog, July 28. www.management-mentors.com/about/corporate-mentoring-matters-blog/bid/67435/Saying-Goodbye-in-Mentoring.

Maslow, A. 1966. *The Psychology of Science.* New York: Harper Collins.

MasterClass. 2018. "James Patterson Teaches Writing." July. www.masterclass.com/classes/james-patterson-teaches-writing.

McCauley, C. 2006. *Developmental Assignments: Creating Learning Experiences Without Changing Jobs.* Greensboro, NC: CCL Press.

McLeod, S. 2018. "Erik Erikson's Stages of Psychosocial Development." *SimplyPsychology.* www.simplypsychology.org/Erik-Erikson.html.

Melton, M. 2017. "Millennials Seem to Be Key to Meal-Kit Subscription Success." *eMarketer Retail,* September 11. https://retail.emarketer.com/article/millennials-seem-key-meal-kit-subscription success/59b6fb54ebd4000a7823ab02.

MentorCloud. 2014. "Mentoring Lessons with IBM's Brenda Dear." MentorCloud, November 3. www.mentorcloud.com/2014/11/03/mentoringlessonswithbrendadea.

Morgan, J. 2016. "Marshall Goldsmith on How to Drive Behavior Change." *Forbes,* June 27. www.forbes.com/sites/jacobmorgan/2016/06/27/marshall-goldsmith-on-how-to-drive-behavior-change.

Morrison, S. 2014. "Masterful Mentoring at Sun Microsystems." *Talent Mangement 360,* December. https://talentmanagement360.com/masterful-mentoring-at-sun-microsystems.

Whitney, D., and A. Trosten-Bloom. 2003. *The Power of Appreciative Inquiry: A Practical Guide to Positive Change.* San Francisco: Berrett-Koehler.

Zachery, L.J. 2012. *The Mentor's Guide: Facilitating Effective Learning Relationships,* 2nd ed. San Francisco: Wiley.

# About the Author

**Wendy Axelrod, PhD,** is a coach, author, speaker, and volunteer. For three decades, both as a corporate HR executive of a Fortune 100 company and external consultant, Wendy has helped organizations substantially increase their development efforts, working with thousands of managers and mentors in workshops and coaching engagements in the United States and internationally. Her expertise is in helping people become exceptional at growing the talent of others.

Wendy's first book, *Make Talent Your Business: How Exceptional Managers Develop People While Getting Results* (co-authored with Jeannie Coyle), identified the five research-based practices that distinguish exceptional developmental managers, helping leaders learn what it truly takes to seamlessly weave development with performance. Experts have already identified her second book, *10 Steps to Successful Mentoring,* as the most complete and practical guide for succeeding with mentoring relationships.

Wendy's works have appeared in *SmartBriefs on Leadership*; AMA's Moving Ahead, Leader to Leader, and Leadership Excellence; the Conference Board's Human Capital Exchange; SHRM's *HR People+Strategy*; and European journals. She has also authored numerous chapters and entries in books such as *The ASTD Management Development Handbook*. She speaks at conferences for organizations including the Association for Talent Development, the Conference Board, Human Resource Planning Society, and HR Summit Asia, as well as corporate events.

Wendy's clients include Fortune 100 companies and medium-sized firms in the United States and globally. Wendy has been a consultant with Korn Ferry and AchieveForum, a faculty member for the Institute for Management Studies (IMS), and a coach for AthenaOnline. As a human resources executive during her 16-year tenure at Sunoco, she led the functions of leadership development, organization change, and talent management and guided a company through a significant multiyear organizational change process.

Passionate about development and professional growth, Wendy is the volunteer creator and moving force behind the Philadelphia region's renowned Mentoring Program for HR Professionals. The program has helped scores of professionals to develop, take on bigger roles, and thrive in more satisfying careers, and in 2017 Wendy was identified as the region's "Mentoring Guru." Over a 20-year period, she has formally served as a mentor to dozens of professionals. Wendy consults with companies to build and strengthen their mentoring programs as a key component of their talent development strategies.

Wendy holds a PhD in organizational and industrial psychology from Colorado State University. She also completed an advanced program in HR management at Columbia University, and she is certified in dozens of executive coaching and organization development tools, including Conversational Intelligence Enhanced Skill Practitioner.

Wendy and her husband live outside Philadelphia and have five children. They love the outdoors (kayaking, hiking, camping) and are avid community and global volunteers. They've even participated in two-week medical missions in developing countries through Rotary International. Find out more about Wendy at www.WendyAxelrodPhD.com

# Index

as part of journaling, 126
promote the habit, 22, 99
to raise awareness of bias, 162
relationship skills
cultivating a positive environment, 19
getting to know your mentee, 92–94
for improving influencing abilities, 146–147
starting a mentoring relationship, 30
resilience, 19–20, 94, 125, 150
resources, using others as, 14–15, 75–77
respect
five *Bes* of respectfully asking questions, 114
mutual respect and trust, 35–36, 95
reverse mentoring, 127–128
rewards for mentors, 2–5
risk-taking, 19–20, 86
roles that develop mentee other than mentor
consultant, 15
external coach, 14
manager-coach, 14
trusted colleague, 15
role of the mentee
mentee behaviors, 43
responsibilities, 41–43
role of the mentor
describing, 13
influence on the mentee, 20–21
others who help develop the mentee, 14–15, 75–77
responsibilities, 38–39
six mentor behaviors, 39–41
role playing or rehearsing, 130–131
rule of reciprocity, 147

## S

safety
conversational safety space, 18, 94–97
feeling comfortable taking risks, 19–20, 86
trust, 87–88, 95, 170
self-awareness
mentee responsibility, 42
raising, 97–99
know yourself, 90, 91
questions that deepen, 107–108
site visits, 128–129
starting where the mentee is currently, 17–18
SWOT analysis tool, 72

## T

technology
to overcome distance issues, 164–165
Thailand cave rescue example of practical psychology, 83–84
thinking things through
eight thinking and planning methods, 72
SWOT analysis tool, 72
trust, 87–88, 95, 170

## U

Ullmen, John, 148

## V

values, importance of, 171–173
valuing differences, 139
variety
importance of different types of development to the mentee's growth, 121–122
importance of different types of development to the mentor's growth, 135–136
videos of experts, 130
visuals, creating, 129
voluntary nature of the mentoring relationship, 13
volunteer work, 132–133

## W

working with a colleague, 132
wrap up mentoring. *See* closure of the mentoring relationship

## Z

Zachery, Lois, 57, 162